C000228684

THE B HATTI

By Samuel Adamson

CAST

James
Charles Edwards

**Bo / Mrs Arbuthnot /
Rosamund /
Louise / Eve /
Madame Schultz**
Suzette Llewellyn

Hattie
Sophie Thompson

Chrissie
Alivia Mihayo
Luna Valentine

Pianist
Berrak Dyer

Alternate Pianist
Maya Irgalina

CREATIVE TEAM

Playwright
Samuel Adamson

Director
Richard Twyman

Designer
Jon Bausor

Lighting Designer
Simisola
Majekodunmi

Sound Designer
Pete Malkin

Composers
Nicola T. Chang
David Shrubsole

Musical Director
David Shrubsole

Movement Director
Anjali Mehra

Casting Director
Lotte Hines CDG

Costume Supervisor
Isobel Pellow

Assistant Director
Zoë Templeman-
Young

PRODUCTION TEAM

**Production
Managers**
Heather Doole
Alysha Laviniere

**Associate
Production Manager**
Charlotte Ranson

**Company
Stage Manager
(Rehearsals)**
Katie Bachtler

**Company
Stage Manager
(Running)**
EJ Saunders

**Deputy
Stage Manager**
Caroline Meer

**Assistant
Stage Manager
(Book Cover)**
Daze Corder

Wardrobe Manager
Ayushi Srivastava

Chaperones
Griffin Chaperones

Technician
Bradley Halliwell

Technician Cover
Allie Hu

Tech ASM
Tim Jan Eichelbaum

Show Crew
Chioma Bayo

Tech Swing
Ella Purvis

**Production
Electrician**
Andy Taylor

**Lighting
Programmer**
Paul Salmon

**Production
Sound Engineer**
Richard Bell

**Production
Carpenter**
Calum Walker

Rigger
Jess Wilson

**Revolve
Programmer**
Daniel Thompson

Set Built by
Steel the Scene
Kiln Theatre
Workshops

SPECIAL THANKS TO:
Maira Canzonieri
Courtney Pianos
James 'Luka'
Goodsall
Michael Jacobs
The Royal College
of Music
School children's
voices: Leandra,
Orlando, Mahaylia,
Ruby, Malaiah,
Shayan and Molly
Scott Handley at
Steeldeck Rentals
National Theatre
Yijin Li

**KILN THEATRE ARE
GRATEFUL FOR THE
SUPPORT OF THE
FOLLOWING FOR THIS
PRODUCTION:**
Foyle Foundation
Jon and NoraLee
Sedmak

CAST

CHARLES EDWARDS
JAMES

Charles Edwards returns to the Kiln, having previously appeared in *The 39 Steps* (also Criterion Theatre and Cort Theatre, New York).

Theatre credits include: *Best Of Enemies* (Young Vic); *Absolute Hell*, *Waste*, *NT50*, *Strange Interlude* (Clarence Derwent Award winner), *This House*, *Twelfth Night*, *All My Sons*, *The Duchess Of Malfi* (National Theatre); *Copenhagen* (Minerva Theatre, Chichester); *My Fair Lady* (Opera Australia – Green Room Award winner); *Richard II*, *Much Ado About Nothing* (Shakespeare's Globe); *Blithe Spirit* (Gielgud Theatre/Ahmanson Theatre, Los Angeles); *The King's Speech* (Wyndham's Theatre); *Wanderlust* (Royal Court Theatre) and *Hay Fever* (Haymarket Theatre Royal).

Television credits include: *The Lord of the Rings: The Rings of Power*, *The Crown*, *Downton Abbey*, *The Terror*, *Henry IX*, *The Halycon*, *Sherlock*, *Arthur and George*, *Ripper Street*, *Trying Again*, *A Young Doctor's Notebook*, and *Holy Flying Circus*.

Film credits include: *The Duke*, *The Witches*, *Florence Foster Jenkins*, *Philomena*, *Batman Begins*, *Diana*, *Relative Values*, *Mansfield Park*, and *An Ideal Husband*.

SUZETTE LLEWELLYN
BO / MRS ARBUTHNOT / ROSAMUND / LOUISE / EVE / MADAME SCHULTZ

Theatre credits include: *Foxes* (59E59); *The Fellowship* (Hampstead Theatre); *Electric Rosary* (Royal Exchange Manchester); *Running with Lions* (Talawa Theatre, Lyric Hammersmith Theatre); *Chigger Foot Boys* (Tara Theatre); *Urban Afro Saxons* (Talawa Theatre) and *Marisol* (Traverse Theatre).

Television credits include: *Vera* (as Louisa Hampton), *Eastenders* (as series regular Sheree Trueman), *Top Boy*, *Doctors* (as series regular Estelle Vere), *Hollyoaks* (as series regular Margaret Smith), *Rocket's Island* and *Black Silk*

Film credits include: *The Mouse*, *Real*, *Faces*, *Baby Mother* and *Playing Away*.

In the 1990s Suzette co-founded the innovative theatre troupe The BiBi Crew. The company was dedicated to producing new writing from an African-Caribbean perspective incorporating, music, dance, comedy and drama. The BiBi Crew toured the UK with *On A Level* and *But Stop! We Have Work To Do* and were invited to perform in New York.

SOPHIE THOMPSON
HATTIE

Theatre credits include: *Present Laughter* (The Old Vic – WhatsOnStage Award for Best Supporting Actress in a Play); *Guys & Dolls* (Savoy Theatre); *Into the Woods* (Donmar Warehouse – Olivier Award For Best Actress in a Musical); *Company* (Donmar Warehouse / Noel Coward Theatre – Clarence Derwent Award); *She Stoops to Conquer* (National Theatre); *Clybourne Park* (Royal Court / Wyndham's); *The Importance of Being Earnest* (Vaudeville Theatre); *Female of the Species* (Vaudeville Theatre) and *Wildest Dreams* (RSC Stratford / Barbican).

Television credits include: *Silo*, *Belgravia: The Next Chapter*, *Sisters*, *Sex Education*, *Sandylands*, *Feelgood*, *Detectorists*, *Coronation Street* (as series regular Rosemary Piper), *Eastenders* (as series regular Stella Crawford), *A Room with a View, The Railway Children* and *Persuasion. Celebrity Masterchef* winner 2014.

Film credits include: *Harry Potter and the Deathly Hallows, Gosford Park, Dancing at Lughnasa, Relative Values, Emma* and *Four Weddings and a Funeral.*

ALIVIA MIHAYO
CHRISSIE

Training: Anna Fiorentini Theatre & Film School, 1:1 singing lessons with Vocal Coach Kirsty Cherrett.

Commercial credits include: *Vanguard* and *Mrs Doubtfire the Musical.*

Alivia is skilled at Commercial and Street dance and attends weekly dance sessions. She is delighted to be making her stage debut in *The Ballad of Hattie and James.*

LUNA VALENTINE
CHRISSIE

Training: New London Performing Arts Centre (NLPAC) and Bodens Performing Arts

Commercial credits include: Luna has filmed various promo videos for Nickelodeon's *Paw Patrol.*

Luna is excited to be making her stage debut! Luna is on Grade 3 Piano (ABRSM) and also enjoys playing the drums and singing. She also loves ballet and tap.

BERRAK DYER
PIANIST

Berrak studied as a soloist and accompanist at the Guildhall School of Music and Drama and then went on to study at the Solti Academy and the National Opera Studio.

Berrak was the Musical Director for Pop Up Opera (2014–18). She has worked extensively in the world of opera, and her credits include: *La Fanciulla del West,*

Lakme, La Traviata, Eugene Onegin (Opera Holland Park); *Snow, Goldilocks and the Three Little Pigs*, conductor for *Robin Hood* (The Opera Story); *Rhondda Rips It Up* (Welsh National Opera); *Eugene Onegin, The Dancing Master* (Buxton International Festival), and as assistant conductor: *Cosi fan Tutte* (ETO); *Psychosis 4.48, Phaedra* and *The Lost Thing* (Royal Opera House). During the 2021 season Berrak joined West Green House Opera with Gigi and Iford Arts on Pagliacci. In 2022 Berrak was MD for *Her Day* Opera in Coventry. She returned to conduct *Beauty and the Seven Beasts* with The Opera Story, the Royal Opera House to assist on *The Blue Woman* and West Green House Opera to play and assist on *L'Elisir D'Amore.*

Projects in 2023 included *Hansel und Gretel* and the world premiere of Jonathan Dove's *Itch*, both at Opera Holland Park, *The Yellow Wall Paper* with The Opera Story and conducting the Opera Scenes at Royal Birmingham Conservatoire. This year Berrak joins the cast of *The Ballad of Hattie and James* at the Kiln Theatre, returns to Opera Holland Park for *Tosca* and then West Green House for *Il Barbiere di Siviglia.*

MAYA IRGALINA
ALTERNATE PIANIST

London-based Maya Irgalina is a Belarusian pianist of Tatar origin. She performs internationally, with UK highlights including Barbican, Wigmore Hall, Machynlleth Festival, Oscar Wilde Weekend, and Cheltenham Jazz Festival.

Maya has won numerous prizes in piano competitions, including Dudley, Sydney, Maria Yudina and Scriabin. She is the winner of the RNCM's highest accolade for solo performance, the Gold Medal, and had her Wigmore Hall debut as a winner of the Worshipful Company of Musicians auditions. Her playing was broadcast by ABC (Australia), BBC Radio 3 and Belarusian Radio.

As a soloist, she has played with orchestras including City of Birmingham Symphony Orchestra, Manchester Camerata, Belarusian Opera House

Orchestra, RNCM Symphony Orchestra, Batumi Symphony Orchestra and others.

As a collaborative pianist, Maya has been selected as Britten-Pears Young Artist and was featured in Semyon Bychkov's Beloved Friend project about Tchaikovsky. She regularly performs with such singers as Fleur Barron, Ruby Philogene and Nicola Said; she has received The Paul Hamburger Prize from Graham Johnson and is an alumna of Franz Schubert Institute in Baden bei Wien, Austria.

Maya is very grateful to her professors Lilia Ter-Minasian, Graham Scott, Ronan O'Hora and Julius Drake. She holds the International Artist Diploma in Solo Performance from the Royal Northern College of Music and the Master's degree in Music from the Guildhall School of Music and Drama.

CREATIVE TEAM

SAMUEL ADAMSON
PLAYWRIGHT

For Kiln: *Wife*

Plays and adaptations for the stage include: *Running Wild* (Chichester Festival Theatre/Regent's Park Open Air Theatre); *My Name is Frida* (Hoard Festival/New Vic Stoke); Chekhov's *Uncle Vanya* (West Yorkshire Playhouse); *The Light Princess*, *Southwark Fair*, Ibsen's *Pillars of the Community*, *Mrs Affleck* (National Theatre); *Gabriel* (Shakespeare's Globe); Ostrovsky's *Larisa and the Merchants*, Schnitzler's *Professor Bernhardi* (Arcola Theatre); *Frank & Ferdinand* (National Theatre Connections); *Decade* (Headlong Theatre); *Some Kind of Bliss* (Trafalgar Studios); *All About My Mother* (Old Vic); *A Chain Play* (Almeida); *Fish and Company* (National Youth Theatre/Soho Theatre); *24 Hour Plays* (Old Vic); Ibsen's *A Doll's House* (Southwark Playhouse); Chekhov's *The Cherry Orchard* (Oxford Stage Company/Riverside Studios); Chekhov's *Three Sisters* (Oxford Stage Company/Whitehall Theatre); *Drink, Dance, Laugh and Lie, Clocks and Whistles* (Bush Theatre) and *Grace Note* (Peter Hall Company/Old Vic).

RICHARD TWYMAN
DIRECTOR

Richard Twyman took up the role of Artistic Director of ETT (English Touring Theatre) in November 2016. He was previously Associate Director (International) at the Royal Court Theatre, where he worked with playwrights across the world to develop their plays. Prior to this, he spent five years at the Royal Shakespeare Company working on fourteen productions including the critically acclaimed and Olivier Award-winning *Histories Cycle*.

Theatre credits include: *Macbeth* (ETT, UK/International Tour); *Othello* (ETT, UK/International Tour); *Dealing with Clair* (ETT/Orange Tree Theatre); *You for Me for You, Torn, Harrogate, The Djinns of Eidgah* (Royal Court); *Henry IV Pt II* (Royal Shakespeare Company); *Ditch* (Old Vic Tunnels); *Les Liaisons Dangereuses* (Theatre Cocoon, Tokyo/Osaka); *Deliver Us* (Theatre De La Ville, Luxembourg); *The Mystery of Charles Dickens* (Playhouse Theatre/UK Tour) and *Give Me Your Hand* (Irish Repertory Theatre, New York).

JON BAUSOR
DESIGNER

Jon Bausor studied Music at Oxford University and Royal Academy of Music before retraining on the Motley Theatre

Design Course. He designed the opening ceremony of the *London 2012 Paralympic Games* and was recently nominated for an Emmy Award for his Production Design on the Redbull film *Human Pinball*. As an Associate Artist of the RSC Jon has designed numerous productions including *Hamlet*, *The Winter's Tale* and the entire 2012 season.

Theatre credits include: *Spirited Away* (London Colosseum); *Bat Out of Hell* (Dominion Theatre / New York City Centre / Paris Theatre, Las Vegas); *Into The Woods* (Bath Theatre Royal); *Spirited Away* (Imperial Theatre, Tokyo / International tour); *The Grinning Man* (Bristol Old Vic / Trafalgar Studio – UK Theatre Award for Best Design); *King Lear* (Wyndham's Theatre); *The James Plays* (National Theatre / National Theatre Scotland / International Tour); *Mametz* (National Theatre Wales – UK Theatre Award and Wales Theatre Award for Best Design); *I am Yusuf* (ShiberHur, Palestine / Young Vic); *Cold War* and *They Drink it in the Congo* (Almeida).

Opera includes: *Ainadamar* (Scottish Opera / Welsh National Opera / Detroit Opera / Metropolitan Opera, New York); *Cendrillon* (Glyndebourne); *The Knot Garden* (Theater an der Wien); *Xerses*; *Rigoletto*, *A Midsummer Night's Dream* (Halle Opera) and *Agrippina* (The Grange Festival).

Jon's extensive dance collaborations include designs for Rambert, Royal Ballet, Norwegian and Finnish National Ballets, Nederlands Dans Theater, and English National Ballet.

SIMISOLA MAJEKODUNMI
LIGHTING DESIGNER

Simisola Majekodunmi trained at the Royal Academy of Dramatic Arts (RADA) and has a degree in Lighting Design.

For Kiln: *Es & Flo* (also Wales Millenium Centre).

Theatre credits include: *A Taste of Honey* (Royal Exchange Theatre); *Metamorphosis* (Frantic Assembly / UK Tour); *I, Daniel Blake* (Northern Stage / UK Tour); *Choir Boy* (Bristol Old Vic); *Sound of the Underground*, *Is God Is*, *Living Newspaper* (Royal Court); *Family Tree* (Belgrade Theatre / UK Tour); *Treason: The Musical in Concert* (Theatre Royal Dury Lane); *J'OUVERT* (Theatre503 / Harold Pinter Theatre) *Starcrossed* (Wilton's Music Hall); *Electric Rosary* (Royal Exchange Theatre); *A Christmas Carol* (Shakespeare North Playhouse); *Nine Night* (Leeds Playhouse); *Human Nurture* (Sheffield Theatres) and *The Wiz* (Hope Mill Theatre).

Dance credits include: *Dark with Excessive Bright* (ROH); *Traplord* (180 Studios); *The UK Drill Project* (Barbican); *Born to Exist* (Netherlands / UK Tour); *AZARA – Just Another Day & Night* (The Place) and *Puck's Shadow* (Watford Palace).

PETE MALKIN
SOUND DESIGNER

Pete Malkin is a Sound Designer for Theatre and Film. He trained at the Royal Central School of Speech and Drama.

Theatre credits include: *A Midsummer Night's Dream* (RSC); *The Time Traveller's Wife* (Apollo Theatre); *Death of England: Closing Time*, *Othello*, *Death of England: Delroy*, *Death of England* (National Theatre); *Let the Right One In*, *There is a Light That Never Goes Out*, *Death of a Salesman* (Royal Exchange Theatre); *Harry Potter and The Cursed Child* (Sonia Friedman Productions); *The Chairs* (Almeida); *Deciphering* (Curious Detective); *Frogman* (Curious Detective / Shoreditch Town Hall / International Tour / Edinburgh Fringe Festival / UK Tour); *Shade* (ThickSkin Theatre); *The Cherry Orchard* (Toneelgroep); *The Unreturning* (Frantic Assembly / UK Tour); *Pity*, *The Kid Stays in the Picture* (Royal Court); *Schism* (Park Theatre); *The Encounter* (Complicité / International Tour / European Tour / Barbican Theatre / John Golden Theatre, New York); *Beware of Pity* (Complicité / Schaubühne / Barbican Theatre); *The Last Testament of Lillian Bilocca* (Hull City of Culture); *The Seagull* (Lyric Hammersmith); *White Bike* (The Space); *The Tempest* (Donmar Warehouse / St Anns Warehouse,

New York/Kings Cross Theatre); *Home Chat* (Finborough Theatre) and *Andrea Chenier* (Opera North/UK Tour).

For *The Encounter*, Pete won a Tony Award for Best Sound Design, a Drama Desk Award for Outstanding Sound Design for a Play, a Helpmann Award for Best Sound Design and an Evening Standard Award for Best Design.

NICOLA T. CHANG
COMPOSER

Nicola T. Chang is a composer and sound designer for stage and screen. She was the composer/sound designer on the 2020/21 *Old Vic 12* cohort and a current BAFTA Connect Member (Film Composer). She was a co-winner of the 2021 Evening Standard Future Theatre Fund (Audio Design).

Theatre credits include: *My Neighbour Totoro, All Mirth and No Matter* (RSC); *For Black Boys Who Have Considered Suicide When the Hue Gets Too Heavy* (Garrick Theatre/Apollo Theatre/Royal Court/New Diorama); *Kerry Jackson* (National Theatre); *Minority Report* (Nottingham Playhouse/Birmingham Rep/Lyric Hammersmith); *Feral Monster* (National Theatre of Wales); *Garden of Words* (Park Theatre); *The Real and Imagined History of the Elephant Man* (Nottingham Playhouse/Blackpool Grand/Belgrade Theatre); *TRIBE, Of the Cut* (Young Vic); *Derren Brown's Unbelievable* (Criterion Theatre/Mercury Colchester/Manchester Palace); *The Ministry of Lesbian Affairs* (Soho Theatre); *The Swell* (Orange Tree); *Little Baby Jesus* (Orange Tree, JMK 2019); *Top Girls* (Liverpool Everyman); *NEST* (LEEDS 2023); *Macbeth* (Leeds Playhouse); *Dziady* (Almeida); *White Pearl* (Royal Court); *Miss Julie* (Chester Storyhouse) and *The Death of Ophelia* (Shakespeare's Globe).

As performer: *Fantastically Great Women Who Changed the World* (Assistant MD/Keys 2/Percussion); *Six the Musical* (Deputy MD/Keys 1); *STOMP* (Ambassador's Theatre/World Tour). She has performed with the Chineke! Orchestra, the Women of the World Orchestra and the London Film Music Orchestra, and at venues such as the Royal Albert Hall, the Royal Festival Hall and Shakespeare's Globe. She currently works with companies including National Youth Theatre, Rambert, British Youth Musical Theatre, National Youth Ballet and House of Absolute.

DAVID SHRUBSOLE
COMPOSER & MUSICAL DIRECTOR

David Shrubsole studied music at Trinity College of Music, and dramaturgy and critical theory at Goldsmiths University.

For Kiln Theatre: *Holy Sh!t, Wife*

Theatre credits include: *Dear Octopus, The Great Wave, My Country: a Work in Progress, The Threepenny Opera, Table, London Road, The Magistrate, She Stoops to Conquer, Major Barbara, The Enchantment, The Alchemist, My Fair Lady* (National Theatre); *Charlie and the Chocolate Factory, Sweeney Todd, Sunshine on Leith, The Crucible, Europe, Dr Korczak's Example, Annie, Peter Pan, Martin Guerre* (Leeds Playhouse); *American Psycho* (Almeida); *The Great Wall* (Singapore Drama Centre); *Porgy and Bess, Romeo and Juliet, Hello Dolly, Much Ado About Nothing* (Regent's Park Open Air Theatre); *A Chorus Line, Assassins, Ain't Misbehavin', Amadeus* (Sheffield Crucible); *Conversations with Coward, Just So, Hayfever* (Chichester Festival Theatre); *Of Mice and Men* (Mercury Theatre Colchester); *Hobson's Choice* (Watermill Theatre); *Total Eclipse* (Menier Chocolate Factory); *You are Here* (Goodspeed Opera House); *Something Wicked This Way Comes* (Delaware Theatre Company); *The Three Musketeers, Troilus and Cressida* (Chicago Shakespeare); *Gaslight* (The Old Vic); *A Streetcar Named Desire* (Clwyd Theatre Cymru/Leicester Curve); *Miss Saigon* (Prince Edward Theatre); *The Wind in the Willows* (London Palladium) and *Epitaph for George Dillon* (Comedy Theatre).

David was awarded the 2017 Drama Desk Award for 'Outstanding Revue' for his work *Life is For Living: Conversations with Coward.*

ANJALI MEHRA
MOVEMENT DIRECTOR

Anjali Mehra is a London-based Movement Director and Choreographer. She trained at Central School of Ballet, London where she won the Christopher Gable Choreographer Award, with a master's degree in Choreography.

Anjali joined Matthew Bourne's New Adventures Dance company in 1999 after graduating from Central School of Ballet, London. She performed on and off with the company over 20 years as a principal dancer in *The Red Shoes*, *Cinderella*, *Swan Lake*, *Nutcracker* and *Play without Words*.

Anjali was in the original cast of *Bombay Dreams* (Apollo Theatre) and *Kiss Me Kate* (Théâtre du Châtelet, Paris).

Recent choreography / movement direction include: *Lord of the Rings*, *A Musical Tale*, *Othello* (also co-director), *Spike*, *Brief Encounter*, *As You Like It (Water Mill Theatre)*; *Flowers for Mrs Harris (Riverside Studios)*; *Daddy* (Almeida); *Judgment Day* (Park Avenue Armoury, New York); *Cherry Town* (Welsh National Opera); *Mavra*, *Pierrot Lunaire* (Royal Opera House); *Jacob Lenz* (English National Opera); *Dick Whittington* (Watford Palace Theatre); *L'Orfeo* (Silent Opera); *God Only Knows* (Tate Modern) and *Rumi The Musical* (London Coliseum).

Anjali directed and choreographed two dance films commissioned by Matthew Bourne's New Adventures – *Moving in Time* and *Little Grasses Crack Through Stone*.

LOTTE HINES CDG
CASTING DIRECTOR

Lotte Hines has worked as a freelancer as well as in-house for Royal Court, Julie Harkin Casting and Kharmel Cochrane Casting.

For Kiln Theatre: *Mlima's Tale*.

As Casting Director, theatre credits include: *Macbeth* (ETT); *Romeo & Juliet*, *Let the Right One in*, *Nora – A Doll's House*, *The Mountaintop*, *Glee & Me* (Royal Exchange Theatre); *Never Have I Ever*, *The Vortex*, *Mom, How Did You Meet The Beatles*, *The Boy in the Striped Pyjamas* (Chichester Theatre); *Accidental Death of an Anarchist* (Haymarket / Lyric Hammersmith / Sheffield Crucible); *Closer*, *Jack and the Beanstalk* (Lyric Hammersmith); *Pride and Prejudice* (Sheffield Crucible); *The Tempest*, *As You Like It*, *Pride and Prejudice* (Regent's Park Open Air Theatre); *Harry Potter and the Cursed Child* (Sonia Friedman Productions); *The Forest* (Hampstead Theatre); *Ivan and the Dogs*, *Thing of Dry Hours*, *La Musica* (Young Vic); *The Dark* (Oval House / UK Tour); *Hole* (Royal Court); *The Wolves* (Theatre Royal Stratford East); *Meek*, *Junkyard*, *Boys Will Be Boys*, *The Absence of War*, *The Glass Menagerie* (Headlong); *People, Places and Things* (UK Tour); *The Barbershop Chronicles* (US Tour); *Elephant* (Birmingham Rep); *Speech and Debate* (Trafalgar Studios); *The Iliad*, *The Weir* (The Lyceum Edinburgh) and *Brenda* (HighTide Festival / The Yard Theatre).

As Casting Director, short film credits include: *Influencers* and *CLA'AM and Above* (Winner of Best Short Film at the National Film Awards).

As Casting Associate, credits include: *Lockwood & Co*, *Lady Chatterley's Lover* (Netflix); *Harry Potter and the Cursed Child* (Sonia Friedman Productions); *The Seagull* (Regent's Park Open Air Theatre); *Tipping the Velvet* (Lyric Hammersmith / Royal Lyceum Theatre Edinburgh) and *Bull* (Sheffield Crucible).

As Casting Assistant, credits include: *Hamlet* (Sonia Friedman Productions / Barbican) and *A View From The Bridge* (Young Vic).

ISOBEL PELLOW
COSTUME SUPERVISOR

Isobel Pellow trained at the London College of Fashion.

For Kiln: *Girl on an Altar*, *Retrograde*, *Mlima's Tale*

Costume Supervision credits include: *Bronco Billy* (Charing Cross Theatre); *HIR* (Park Theatre); *Jack and the Beanstalk*

(Stratford East); *The Walworth Farce* (Southwark Playhouse Elephant); *A Christmas Carole* (Southend Palace); *Alice in Wonderland* (Brixton House); *House of Flamenka* (Peacock Theatre); *The Memory of Water, Blackout Songs* (Hampstead Theatre); *Urinetown* (Royal Academy of Music); *Green Eggs and Ham* (Opera North); *The Sweet Science of Bruising, Britten in Brooklyn* (Wilton's Music Hall); *The Crowning of Poppea* (Hampstead Garden Opera / Jackson's Lane Theatre); *Five Plays* (Young Vic); *Four Play and Clickbait* (Theatre 503).

Costume Design credits include: *Twelfth Night* (Theatre on Kew); *The Lay of the Land* (The Place); *Death Drop* (Criterion Theatre / UK Tour); *Yes So I Said Yes, Not Quite Jerusalem, The Wind of Heaven* (Finborough Theatre); *Lysistrata* (The Cockpit); *Heather and Harry* (Camden People's Theatre); *King Lear* (Pleasure Dome Theatre Company); *'Tis Pity She's a Whore* (Tristan Bates Theatre); *Tales of Offenbach* (Opera Della Luna at Wilton's Music Hall); *Three Brothers* (Theatre N16); *The Xmas Carol* (Old Red Lion); *Sense and Sensibility, Mary Stuart, A Streetcar Named Desire* (Oxford Playhouse); *Blue Stockings, Hay Fever* (Old Fire Station Theatre, Oxford) and *The Accrington Pals* (Ashcroft Theatre, Croydon).

ZOË TEMPLEMAN-YOUNG
ASSISTANT DIRECTOR

Zoë Templeman-Young trained as an actor before becoming a freelance director in 2017. She was a Jerwood Assistant Director at the Young Vic and during her time there worked on *Hamlet* (Associate Director) and *The Collaboration* (Director on placement). Her credits include the newly commissioned play from Marina Carr, *DEMETER* (Young Vic, 5 Shorts), *A Very Quiet Voice* and *46 Jews* (Emanate Productions at Kiln Theatre) and a new adaptation of Philip Pulman's *The Book of Dust: La Belle Sauvage* with Bryony Lavery for Royal Welsh College of Music and Drama. Her other productions at RWCMD include *Angels in America* and *Indecent*. She is a dramaturg and published playwright with her award-winning verbatim play *Take Care*. Zoë is also a tutor and mentor for young adults wanting to get into acting, as well as a mentor at Tunbridge Wells Welcomes Refugees.

K L N

"Kiln Theatre has revitalised the cultural life of Brent and brings world-class theatre at an affordable price to people from all walks of life." **Zadie Smith**

Kiln Theatre sits in the heart of Kilburn in Brent, a unique and culturally diverse area of London where over 150 languages are spoken. We are a welcoming and proudly local venue, with an internationally acclaimed programme of world and UK premieres. Our work presents the world through a variety of lenses, amplifying unheard and ignored voices into the mainstream, exploring and examining the threads of human connection that cross race, culture and identity.

"This place was a special cocoon. Now she has grown and blossomed into a beautiful butterfly." **Sharon D Clarke**

We believe that theatre is for all and want everyone to feel welcome and entitled to call Kiln their own. We are committed to nurturing the talent of young people and adults from local communities, providing a platform for their voices to be heard.

"I wanted to say thank you for creating the most diverse theatre I have been to. In terms of race, culture, class, age, everything – not only in the selection of shows and actors, but in the audience." **Audience member**

Welcome to Kilburn.

Kiln Theatre, 269 Kilburn High Road, London, NW6 7JR
KilnTheatre.com | info@KilnTheatre.com
🅵 🅾 𝕏 ▶ 🅾 @KilnTheatre

 Supported by **ARTS COUNCIL ENGLAND**   Registration No. 1396429. Registered Charity No. 276892

ETT (English Touring Theatre) is a UK-based international touring company. Founded in 1993, this year will see ETT celebrating 30 years of staging both new and classic productions of outstanding quality, imagination, and ambition, which have played to audiences across the globe. ETT makes innovative and pioneering immersive digital experiences; work which interrogates and celebrates contemporary England, reinventing the rules, and reflecting the diversity of the nation. You can find our work in your local theatre, online, at festivals, in a field, internationally and in the West End.

In the last five years ETT has produced over 50 live productions and pieces of digital work, enjoyed by audiences of over 340,000; and has won the UK Theatre Awards Best Touring Production in 2014, 2015, 2016; Best New Play Revival in 2019; Excellence in Inclusivity and Best Play in 2022; and Excellence in Touring 2023.

Alongside *The Ballad of Hattie and James*, ETT is co-producing Kate Attwell's *Testmatch* with Orange Tree Theatre & Octagon Theatre Bolton; touring immersive XR experience *Museum of Austerity* directed by Sacha Wares; touring *Abigail's Party* directed by RTST Award winner Jack Bradfield, and taking *Macbeth*, directed by Richard Twyman, to the Lyric Hammersmith in 2025.

To find out more please go to **ett.org.uk**, where you can sign up to our mailing list and discover how you can be a part of ETT's future.

SUPPORT KILN THEATRE

As a charity, we rely on donations from our audience members and our community of supporters to achieve our mission: to make theatre for all.

We need your help to stage our internationally renowned, representative and bold theatre programme, to inspire the next generation of theatremakers, and to ensure that everyone can experience the power of theatre through our work with local communities.

We want everyone to feel entitled to our space and to feel empowered by their engagement with us.

DONATIONS

Donations of all sizes play a crucial role in enabling our work to continue. There are many ways you can support us, from making a donation when booking a ticket, signing up for a regular donation each month, or giving a major gift. You can also support us through your company, Trust or Foundation.

KILN CIRCLE

The Kiln Circle is a philanthropic supporters group that sits at the heart of our theatre. The Circle are given special opportunities to get close to the work on our stage and the artists involved in each of our productions. Donations start from £2,500 per year.

US TAXPAYERS

If you are a US taxpayer and wish to make a tax-effective donation to Kiln Theatre (registered charity number 276892), you can do so easily in dollars through CAF America. CAF America has full 501©(3) status, increasing the tax efficiency of your gift.

For information on supporting Kiln, please visit **KilnTheatre.com/give**

You can also get in touch with Catherine Walker and Liz McCaffry Payne at **020 7625 0135** or **catherineandliz@kilntheatre.com**

Registered with
FUNDRAISING
REGULATOR

Registered Charity No. 276892

THANK YOU

Kiln depends on donations of all sizes to ensure we can fulfil our mission to champion unheard and ignored voices and to make theatre for everyone. We would not be able to continue our work without the support of the following:

STATUTORY FUNDERS

Arts Council England
The National Lottery Heritage Fund
Brent Warm Spaces

COMPANIES

The Agency (London) Ltd
Bloomberg Philanthropies
Investec
Nick Hern Books
Vogue World Fund

MAJOR DONORS AND KILN CIRCLE

The Basden Family
Primrose and David Bell
Torrence Boone
Moyra McGarth Brown
Jules and Cheryl Burns
Mary and Jim Callaghan
Laure Zanchi Duvoisin
Dasha Epstein
Gary and Carol Fethke
Matthew Greenburgh and Helen Payne
Ros and Alan Haigh
Mary Clancy Hatch
Linda Keenan
Adam Kenwright
Jonathan Levy and Gabrielle Rifkind
Brian and Clare Linden
Frances Magee
Dame Susie Sainsbury
Tim and Cathy Score

Jon and NoraLee Sedmak
Dr Miriam Stoppard

INDIVIDUALS AND LEGACIES

Cas Donald
Sue Fletcher
Nazima Kadir and Karl Gorz
Frances Lynn
In memory of Harry Frank Rose
Ann and Peter Sprinz
Sarah and Joseph Zarfaty

TRUSTS AND FOUNDATIONS

29th May 1961 Charitable Trust
The Atkin Foundation
The Austin and Hope Pilkington Trust
Backstage Trust
Bertha Foundation
Chapman Charitable Trust
Christina Smith Foundation
City Bridge Foundation—London's biggest independent charity funder
Cockayne Grants for the Arts, a donor advised fund held at the London Community Foundation
John S Cohen Foundation
The D'Oyly Carte Charitable Trust

Esmée Fairbairn Foundation
The Foyle Foundation
Garfield Weston Foundation
The Garrick Charitable Trust
The Hobson Charity
Jack Petchey Foundation
John Lyon's Charity
John Thaw Foundation
The Mackintosh Foundation
Marie-Louise von Motesiczky Charitable Trust
The Noël Coward Foundation
Pears Foundation
Richard Radcliffe Trust
The Roddick Foundation
Royal Victoria Hall Foundation
Stanley Thomas Johnson Foundation
Theatre Artists Fund Pilot Programme
Three Monkies Trust
The Vanderbilt Family Foundation

And all those who wish to remain anonymous.

FOR KILN THEATRE

The Ballad of Hattie and James

Samuel Adamson's plays and adaptations include: *Jack Maggs* (State Theatre Company South Australia); *Wife* (Kiln Theatre); *The Light Princess*, *Southwark Fair*, *Mrs Affleck*, *Frank & Ferdinand*, *Pillars of the Community* (National Theatre); *Running Wild* (Chichester Festival Theatre/ Regent's Park Open Air Theatre); *Gabriel* (Shakespeare's Globe); *Fish and Company* (Soho Theatre/National Youth Theatre); *Clocks and Whistles* (Bush Theatre); *Drink, Dance, Laugh and Lie* (Bush/Channel 4); *Grace Note* (Peter Hall Company/Old Vic); *Some Kind of Bliss* (Trafalgar Studios); *Tomorrow Week* (BBC Radio 3); *All About My Mother* (Old Vic); as well as original contributions to: *Hoard* (New Vic, Stoke); *24 Hour Plays* (Old Vic); *A Chain Play* (Almeida); *Urban Scrawl* (Theatre503) and *Decade* (Headlong). Versions include: *A Doll's House* (Southwark Playhouse); *Uncle Vanya* (West Yorkshire Playhouse); *The Cherry Orchard*, *Three Sisters* (Oxford Stage Company); *Professor Bernhardi* and *Larisa and the Merchants* (Arcola).

also by Samuel Adamson from Faber

WIFE
GABRIEL
DRINK, DANCE, LAUGH AND LIE
SOME KIND OF BLISS
SOUTHWARK FAIR
MRS AFFLECK
RUNNING WILD
ALL ABOUT MY MOTHER
(Almodóvar)
PILLARS OF THE COMMUNITY
(Ibsen)
LARISA AND THE MERCHANTS
(Ostrovsky)
THE LIGHT PRINCESS
UNCLE VANYA
(Chekhov)

published by Amber Lane Press
CLOCKS AND WHISTLES
GRACE NOTE

published by Samuel French
THREE SISTERS (Chekhov)
THE CHERRY ORCHARD (Chekhov)
A DOLL'S HOUSE (Ibsen)

published by Oberon
PROFESSOR BERNHARDI (Schnitzler)

published by Methuen
FRANK & FERDINAND
(*in* CONNECTIONS 2011)

published by Nick Hern Books
RECOLLECTIONS OF SCOTT FORBES
(*in* DECADE)

SAMUEL ADAMSON

The Ballad of Hattie and James

faber

First published in 2024
by Faber and Faber Limited
The Bindery, 51 Hatton Garden
London, EC1N 8HN

Typeset by Brighton Gray
Printed and bound in the UK by CPI Group (Ltd), Croydon CR0 4YY

A CIP record for this book
is available from the British Library

ISBN 978-0-571-39109-7

MIX
Paper | Supporting
responsible forestry
FSC® C013604

Printed and bound in the UK on FSC® certified paper in line with our continuing
commitment to ethical business practices, sustainability and the environment.
For further information see faber.co.uk/environmental-policy

2 4 6 8 10 9 7 5 3 1

Acknowledgements

Thanks to Richard Porter and my parents; to Richard Twyman; to Katie Haines; to Amit Sharma, Tom Wright, Jennifer Bakst, and everyone at Kiln Theatre and ETT; to the actors who participated in readings; to Sirine Saba, David Shrubsole, Dominic Dromgoole, Linda Nottingham, Tori Amos, Alex Michaelides, Charles Edwards, Sophie Thompson, Suzette Llewellyn, Raffaella Hilty, Guy Kitchenn, Debbie Burridge, Rachel Wagstaff, Simmy Grover, Anthea Cottee, and Terence Dooley; to Maira Canzonieri at the Royal College of Music; and to Indhu Rubasingham.

For Emma McEwin

The **Ballad of Hattie and James** was first presented at Kiln Theatre, London, on 11 April 2024, in a Kiln Theatre and English Touring Theatre co-production. The cast was as follows:

James Charles Edwards
Bo/Mrs Arbuthnot/Rosamund/Louise/Eve/Madame Schultz Suzette Llewellyn
Hattie Sophie Thompson
Chrissie Alivia Mihayo and Luna Valentine

Pianist Berrak Dyer
Alternate Pianist Maya Irgalina

Director Richard Twyman
Designer Jon Bausor
Lighting Designer Simisola Majekodunmi
Sound Designer Pete Malkin
Composers Nicola T. Chang and David Shrubsole
Musical Director David Shrubsole
Movement Director Anjali Mehra
Casting Director Lotte Hines CDG
Costume Supervisor Isobel Pellow
Assistant Director Zoë Templeman-Young

Characters

Hattie

James

Chrissie

Bo

Mrs Arbuthnot

Rosamund

Louise

Eve

Madame Schultz

THE BALLAD OF HATTIE AND JAMES

'Do you talk a great deal to Maurice?' Richard asked.

'All day and half the night, sometimes.'

'What on earth do you talk about?'

'Sex, jealousy, friendship and music, and about the boats sometimes, the right way to prime the pump, and things like that.'

Penelope Fitzgerald, Offshore

Notes

Hattie and James are played by two adult actors of any age, who look the same age.

Bo and the other women are played by one actor who can look the same age as Hattie and James, but preferably older – and not younger.

Chrissie is six to seven.

*

Hattie and James are excellent pianists. The actors don't need to play: have fun with a big box of theatre tricks.

The grand piano can move with elegance and take everything thrown at it.

Act One

A busy London railway station. A rolling indicator board:

Chrissie, in a timeless red duffel coat, is at the public piano picking out a falling semitone figure, oscillating one note to the other. Hattie, distant, minding suitcases, is watching. She is drawn towards the child.

Hattie Can I play with you?

Chrissie (*retreats, scared*)

Hattie Chrissie?

The child runs away. Hattie sits at the piano. She stares. She plays uncertainly. She grows in confidence. The music is lush and beguiling, at first major key and conventionally harmonic, then more complex. It becomes intense. Passengers film with smartphones. Bo enters holding take-away coffees, sees the abandoned suitcases, sees Hattie. Near the climax of a bravura passage, Hattie's hands rise,

Bo Hattie?

and James, in cardigan and cords, is in a different place, staring at his smartphone,

James Hats.

and the piano music continues from his phone, as if uninterrupted. The piano is on the move, the indicator board rolls backwards through time,

SEPTEMBER 1976

17

*and the piano stops in a shaft of light on the stage of
a school hall. The hum of children's voices. Anoraky
James, wearing a blazer and glasses, is studying a score
ostentatiously. Hattie approaches, wearing a blazer from
a different school.*

Hello! First day of rehearsals, don't know what to say, I'm
James, the pianist.

Hattie Hello. Hats. Hattie: Hats: the pianist.

James I am! Well, along with Mrs Arbuthnot from your
school. Two pianists.

Hattie Gosh. But only one piano.

James I know! *Mysterioso.* (*With score.*) The piano part's
a duet. Four hands.

Hattie Gosh.

James I know! Mr Simpson was going to play – (*points out
front*) have you met him yet, our Head of Music? – but the
score arrived, I said, I can play this, so he handed on the
torch. A star is born. Bye-bye Salieri, hello Mozart. (*Laughs,
jokes die.*)

Hattie How old are you?

James Sixteen. Lower Sixth.

Hattie Fuck.

James Y-you?

Hattie Same. Fuck.

James C-c-could you introduce me to Mrs Arbuthnot?

Hattie No. Cover me? (*Stashes vodka bottle from her satchel
inside piano.*)

James S-so are you playing the Recorder, or Slung Mugs,
or – what are you doing?

Hattie Little something to survive the Flood. (*Duh-dums* Jaws-*like rising semitone figure.*)

James Is that alcohol?!

Hattie This hall smells like scrotums.

James Um. I should prepare – Benjamin Britten's very complex – you should go and um – mingle – if you ever need help with the Slung Mugs or – just ask, I'm the Deputy Musical Director.

Hattie Are you? No one told me *that*.

James Yes, when Mr Simpson's sick I deputise.

Hattie Has Mr Simpson got cancer?

James No. But in the event. (*Disconcerted. Pause.*) The Slung Mugs, by the way, are teacups. It's a wonderfully idiosyncratic orchestration. We sling mugs on a piece of string, and the sort of Not-So-Musical People hit them with wooden spoons, thus – (*Demonstrates, sounds notes.*) To create the impression of rain. For Noah's Flood.

Hattie It is thrilling to be alive.

James It was my idea! To programme it! During Maths I actually heard The Voice of God: 'James, This Year's Combined Schools' Musical Cannot Be *Annie Get Your Gun.*' I went straight to Mr Simpson: 'We *have* to do *Noye's Fludde*' and he said, fine, James, you win. Benjamin Britten's my favourite composer. You'll see. He's like um Essence of England.

Hattie Fuck off. A flood? – we've just had a fucking heatwave. And why don't we do a Christmas show about miners' strikes or the IRA?

James Well, it's based on a Chester Mystery Play, so if that's some point about *relevance*, it's been *relevant* for five hundred / years –

Hattie Teacups and hymns and sea shanties, nostalgic bollocks.

James There are no sea shanties, that's *Peter Grimes* and they're sea *interludes*. I can't talk to you about this – go and – y-you should listen to some music that isn't David Cassidy and David Bowie and *Top of the* – this is why we're here, th-this is important extracurricular consolation for *those of us who* – (*Panic attack? Asthma? Re: vodka.*) Get rid of it! (*Heads off.*)

Hattie I'm not Slung Mugs, I'm Piano. Primo.

James I'm primo.

Hattie I thought you were secondo.

James Mrs Arbuthnot is secondo!

Hattie Bye-bye Salieri, hello Mozart.

James (*speechless*)

Hattie I don't want to play with you either, Piggy! (*Points.*) But it is fun to see how much it's eating Mrs Arbuthnot's soul. The crab, in green. You should thank me. Arbuthnot doesn't play the piano, she rapes it.

James (*speechless*)

Hattie We heard some boy-prodigy here had been promoted so it was a matter of school pride.

James D-does Mr Simpson know about this?! Have you seen this score, Benjamin Britten's very complex! There are the children's parts, the plinkety hand-bells and things, then there's th-the *soul*. Who have you studied with, I hope you're miles past diploma level, why wasn't I / told?! –

Hattie (*swipes paperback from his blazer pocket*)

James – give that back! –

Hattie Ted? I prefer Sylvia. (*Flings it away.*)

James – I have to speak to / Mr Simpson –

She plays several bars of Fanny Mendelssohn Hensel's Mélodie op. 4, no. 2, beautifully, as he scrambles for his paperback. She improvises a 1970s finish, glances at teachers, puts head in piano, swigs vodka.

Hattie Played all my life. We have a Bechstein at home.

James A Bechstein? A grand?

Hattie My mother's. When I get a place at the Royal College of Music it's mine. Has your mummy fucked up your life by mapping out your whole fucking life?

James Yes: she's dead.

Hattie Oh. Sorry.

James What was that music?

Hattie Mendelssohn.

James Mendelssohn?

Hattie Fanny Mendelssohn. Felix's sister.

James Yes. Of course. Fanny.

Hattie Fanny, James, Fanny.

Chrissie in a third school's uniform tears towards him.

Chrissie Jamie!

James (*sotto, furious*) Buzz off, Chrissie! (*Can't help being polite.*) This is Hattie.

Hattie Hats.

Chrissie (*to her*) I'm going to be a bird on Noah's Ark, a Dove! (*To him.*) Gavin's an Otter, and Nisha's a Heron and Gavin said it's stupid because why do Nisha and me even need to go on the Ark because we can just fly?

James Nisha and *I*: I don't know, Chrissie, the non-singing Animals are not my Department.

Hattie Tell Gavin if he's an Otter to fucking swim.

Chrissie (*giggles, thrilled. To James, re: piano*) Can I play?

James (*sotto*) I told you to pretend not to know me!

Chrissie My brother's sixteen, he's the deputy something, he plays fantastic!

Hattie I know, he told me.

James *Half*-brother. And I play fantastic*ally*.

Loudhailer Voice Keston Primary girls and boys over here please – that's all forty-nine species of Animal – including you, Christina Culler, off the stage –

Chrissie (*hugs James guilelessly*) Bye! (*Hugs Hattie.*) Bye, Hats!

Hattie (*taken aback; returns affection*) Bye, Chrissie.

The child runs away. He pretends to busy himself with his score. She enjoys his embarrassment.

James D-did she say *dove*? She's not *the* dove, you know *the Dove* that gets the olive branch, she's definitely not the *actual* th-this is all my stepmother's fault, interfering *dragon*, she rang Mr Simpson and asked him to ask Keston Primary to participate –

Hattie Keston Primary participates every fucking year. (*Points.*) Who's that?

James Um. Charlie Tyler.

Hattie Charlie Stunner. Introduce me.

James No, he's a footballer, he doesn't have language.

Hattie He doesn't need language. The old woman?

James Miss Simpson, Mr Simpson's sister, she's twenty-two. (*Both find this ancient.*) He's roped her in especially to play Noah's Wife, we're meant to be amazed she works at the BBC but does that mean she can sing twentieth-century opera?

Hattie And there's Benjamin Britten: a chorus of boys plunking a few teacups, no one gives a shit about the girls, the Ark is steered by adults. A male Establishment bourgeois Middle England old people's plot.

James (*presses score on her*) Yet by our talent you and I are playing the piano duet.

Hattie Talent? – you think these wankers don't live to kill talent, they're scared shitless of us, everyone old's scared of the young, you're scared of your sister.

James You don't know anything about me and my *half*-sister! –

Hattie I know you can't bear she's going to steal the show as the Dove, *Jamie*.

James – as for Miss Simpson I don't care she's old, Noah's Wife *is*, it wouldn't be true to life if the part were played by someone the wrong age, I'm just cross because I didn't get to audition any of you!

Hattie Jesus Christ, forty days and forty fucking nights of this?

James If only! We only have nineteen rehearsals!

Hattie Who cares, it's not as if Benjamin Britten's going to come.

James He might, I invited him, I wrote to him at his house in Aldeburgh, Suffolk.

Hattie (*drops score*) I'm going for a fag with Charlie Tyler.

James (*scrambles for it*) You do that, he's not here for the music, *it's only cos he wants to finger a girl like you*!

He's on the ground. Wretched, apologetic. A strange, silent state of their own.

It-it's a metaphor. I mean I know the whole Bible's a metaphor but it's post-war, it's about how nothing's in ruins forever, it's about, you know, being on the c-c-cusp of life again, so if you want it to be about I dunno a united Ireland, we can find that in it, (*with score*) when the Flood's over and the Animals sing Alleluia here it's not nostalgia, it's hope, we can make it about whatever we want, which isn't true of *Annie Get Your stupid* . . . (*Trails off, upset.*) I'm trying to do what you want . . . I'm just trying to do something a bit real and interesting in this bloody school. (*Pause.*) I hate Christmas.

Hattie You should try spending it watching my fucking parents getting (*gesturing drinking*) fucking plastered in their fucking shack in fucking France.

James Oh France, what a tribulation for you.

Hattie (*smiles. Pause*) I'm happy to be here, all right? (*Takes score.*) And I'm more a composer than pianist, so I'm very happy to be doing this not *Annie Get Your Gun*. Obviously you're the only person in this room I have anything in common with or want to spend more than a second with. Even if you are too thick to realise Charlie Tyler and his mates are never going to be able to sing your favourite opera.

James (*excited*) I know, it's very antiphonal! He can play hand-bells or bang the teacups. (*At music with her.*) There really is something in it for everyone.

Hattie Yeah. I like that about it. There's a lot I like. This Lydian B-flat.

James Yes, Britten loves the Lydian mode. Honestly, it's so good. Actually it's not my favourite opera of his, that's *Death in Venice*.

Hattie And what's that about?

James It's about death. In Venice.

Hattie When I go to Venice I'm going to fucking *live*.

James (*laughs, thrilled*) Are you working on something new? If you're a composer.

Hattie Come for a fag.

James I'm not really a fag sort of person.

Hattie Aren't you? In your NHS spectacles.

James Have we met?

Hattie No: you're unforgettable. Do you want to play primo or secondo, James?

James I don't mind, Hats, you choose.

Hattie I'm primo then. I hope you can take my tempo.

Room hum returns as they begin the opening chords – but the imperious Mrs Arbuthnot strides towards them. She has a loudhailer.

Mrs Arbuthnot Go and introduce yourself to Mr Simpson and Miss Simpson, Hattie, she's a secretary at the BBC, she's here to play Noah's Wife.

Hattie This is their famous pianist James, Mrs Arbuthnot – James, this is our *cunt*ry-church lady organist Mrs Arbuthnot.

She meets Mrs Arbuthnot's furious glare.

Mrs Arbuthnot So it's all your fault? James, James, where is the melody?

Hattie leaves, chanting that rhythmic A. A. Milne-ish phrase behind Mrs Arbuthnot's back: 'James-James-Where-Is-The-Melody-Weatherby-George-Dupree', etc.

James I, I didn't know this would happen, Mrs Arbuthnot –

Mrs Arbuthnot Oh for goodness' sake as if I'd want to play this modern fribble?! (*At piano, peers at music.*) We all know what *Ben*jamin *Britt*en stands for. You're about to put ninety-nine per cent of these children off music for life. (*Opening chords – church-lady organist.*) Out of tune.

James No: it's not. I have perfect pitch.

Mrs Arbuthnot Yes. Of course you do.

Attacks piano again: a scale. Something obstructs a note. He knows what.

James That's a broken hammer. Mr Simpson's getting someone to fix it tomorrow.

Mrs Arbuthnot (*lifts lid, finds vodka, opens it, sniffs it*)

James Tha-tha-that's um – mine.

Mrs Arbuthnot Yours?

James My sister's . . . mother's . . . my half-sister's mother Rosamund, she um (*gestures drinking, like Hattie*) and it upsets my half-sister so she . . . steals Rosamund's . . .

Mrs Arbuthnot (*close*) It's for the best. Hattie Buchanan would have obliterated you.

James ?

Mrs Arbuthnot Ripped your heart out, diced it into little, lonely lumps.

Pupils' laughter: unrelated but he takes it personally.

(*Through loudhailer.*) Boys and girls, THIS IS THE VOICE OF GOD! (*Laughs like God.*) Welcome to our combined schools' production for Christmas 1976, *Noye's Fludde*!

Excitement, sincere and mocking. She exits after Hattie. Chrissie tears towards the piano –

Chrissie Gavin tried to hit me because he wants to be the Dove! Where's Hats? HATS!

Mrs Arbuthnot (*through loudhailer*) SILENCE, ANIMALS!

– silence, except from Chrissie, who plays a falling semitone figure, oscillating –

James Chrissie! Stop!

– but his real concern is Hattie's fate. As he looks her way, the lush and beguiling piano music creeps in, and we now

*hear that Chrissie's restless semitone figure is buried as an
ostinato in the tune itself, so for all her two-fingered
gaucheness, she is in uncanny duet with it. The piano is on
the move and stops in the depths of a public foyer. The
hum of children's voices. Hattie and James at a table in
a shaft of light. No blazers, though he has a satchel-like
bag. He wears his cardigan. She sips tea. He nurses wine.
He often looks at her. She rarely looks at him. Silence.*

Fancy a shag?

Hattie Not in front of the children, darling.

Silence.

James Fancy a shag – in the loos?

Hattie You want toilet sex?

James Yes. Yes I do.

Silence. He drinks.

Piss.

*A child screams – play, but mistaken by both, at first, as
distress.*

I hate it here. Utter dump.

Hattie I love it. It's always packed with kids playing . . .
parents . . . no one cares that up those stairs is a concert hall.
The building's purpose . . . isn't its purpose.

James I hate kids. (*Stabs air with index fingers, squashing
people.*) And parents. And all these other wankers – not you,
I love you – oh good, I've done it. Stressful morning.
Vomiting cat, traffic, other – stuff – and all I could think was:
don't cock it up today. Tell her, at last. (*Pause.*) Well, we can't
keep seeing each other like this without it being said, Hats.
I love you more than I've loved anyone.

*Waits. Mouths/gestures, 'This is where you say it back.'
Nothing.*

I'll take that as Love You Too – come *on*, sex in the bogs, everyone does it here, *that* is *purpose* of the Royal Festival Hall.

Gulps the terrible wine. Long silence.

Your wife is going to get arrested if she keeps lurking over there by the gift shop like that.

JANUARY 2020

Hattie (*calls on smartphone*) He says you look like a paedophile.

James I didn't *quite* say – and you can walk ten metres and talk / to her –

Hattie It's fine, I won't be long, the bookshop downstairs,

James – she can stay, or go, I'd prefer go, it's the in-between / that's –

Hattie Bye. (*Sips tea.*) She worries about me.

James Why? You're with *me* –

Hattie We don't know you from that chair.

James – and why won't you be long? I want us to be *long*.

Silence. Wife obviously leaves because he waves sarcastically, mouths 'Bye'. He stares.

Seeing you again, it's – [mind-blowing]. Well, obviously I've *seen* you, but – in the flesh, to actually – you smell fabulous by the way, and you haven't changed one bit.

Hattie (*stares*) I'm married.

James There's that.

Hattie Whole sections of me are different, I have bits of other people inside of me.

James ?

28

Hattie We have a daughter, Frances, she's at Cambridge. We have an allotment and rent a beach hut in Hastings, normally we'd be there by now, listening to Radio Four, gazing over the Channel. This year I've worked for the Inland Revenue for eighteen years.

James Golly. Congrats.

Hattie On losing my life to the tax office?

James I'm sure you haven't lost your life to it –

Hattie Absolutely I have, doesn't matter, happens to lots of people. What about you, James? Have you changed? –

James When you say – bits of other people – ?

Hattie You've been wearing those corduroys since 'Wuthering Heights'.

James Wow. Bit rude. (*Pause.*) Kate Bush or Emily Brontë?

Hattie I'm surprised you know who Kate Bush is.

James I live for Kate Bush, *I* introduced *you* to –

– she glares; perhaps he parodies 'Wuthering Heights'; he indicates 'Gotcha'. Pause.

You turn twenty. Thirty. Sixty . . . periodically what you're wearing aligns with fashion.

Hattie Not this year.

James I'm a dinosaur. I'm . . . an Emilybrontësaurus (*laughs at terrible pun* –) oh for the love of – she's back – she's actually done a circle – it's all right, I'm not going to steal your precious cargo!

Hattie Cargo?

James I don't mean – it's just – you're my *oldest*, *dearest* – I haven't seen you for *twenty* – can't she give us *five* – do you know who she reminds me of? Mrs Arkwright. You married

Mrs Arkwright. (*Pause.*) You know . . . music teacher from your school – fingers like (*piano playing: fists*) – Arkwright.

Hattie (*pause*) The lesbian?

James Was she?

Hattie Jesus. She must have died with Thatcher.

James Mrs Arkwright was gay?

Hattie The one you snitched to about my vodka?

James What? No –

Hattie Bulldyke, that's why she hated me so much.

James Vodka? Me? I / didn't –

Hattie Mrs Arkwright! God! Was that her name? She was one of those *really evil* 1970s sadists – she's nothing like Mrs Arkwright!

James Oh but she is: yes, I can picture you under the power of your evil schoolmistress wife, luring Hansels and Gretels into your hut by the sea with strawberries from the allotment so she can suck their blood to stay young – oh, she's off on another lap, bye-bye, whatever-your-name-is –

Hattie Bo.

James – Bo, *sweet*, where did you two lovebirds *meet*?

Hattie The City, I'd come out of a job interview, I was off my face, I was about to be run over on Cannon Street, I'd gone to the interview off my face, she helped me, she bought me a chicken sandwich and took me into a church to calm me down, St Mary-le-Bow, that's why I call her Bo, but then the organist started practising, Mendelssohn, it was close to Christmas and I can't stand Felix Mendelssohn so I ran off to drown myself in the Thames, but she followed and kind of attacked me by pulling me into a cab and twenty-one years later I still love her more than I've loved anyone.

James speechless. Silence.

Fuck me. I'd forgotten the tattoo.

James What? Oh. (*On underside of wrist, say.*) Yeah.

Hattie You. Of all the spods.

James Yeah. Drunk in Venice. It's a gondola.

Hattie Is it?

James Or a sort of . . . oriental slipper.

Hattie A racist tattoo.

James Mistake of my life.

Hattie Well, one of them.

She stares. He holds it, just.

James *You* called *me.*

Hattie No, James. You called me.

James No . . . that's *not* . . .

He trails off. Looks away. She keeps staring. Softens.

Hattie What's your cat called?

James Gustav von Aschenbach.

Hattie Oh you silly cunt. (*Pause.*) How's Brooklyn?

James Brooklyn? Went once. Week later the World Trade Center fell down. (*Pause.*) Do you mean – Jerzy?

Hattie Jersey? Jerzy! – with a zed! Tell me you didn't marry Jerzy?

James Reader, I did.

Hattie (*noise!*) Just because we can, James, doesn't mean we should.

James ?!

Hattie The fitness instructor?

James He became a psychotherapist actually!

Hattie No. The feather-brain? That twink? The one you bought a house for in Suffolk?

James Suffolk? I – no, I, I *had* a house in Suffolk – but not for / years –

Hattie Blackheath?

James Yes, Blackheath, I'm still there – y-you should come for supper tonight, in fact why don't you divorce Beach Hut Bo and move in, I could do with the rent, you won't have to grow your own strawberries, I get mine from Waitrose – *and* there's a piano, you don't have one of *those* in the Hastings hut or wherever your house-made-of-bricks is, do you? – no, I knew *that*.

Hattie Your Bechstein.

James What? No, a – keyboard –

Hattie I remember you had – it was in a studio – a Bechstein grand.

James Oh you remember – Jesus, that's a *long* – that wasn't worth the repair / bills,

Hattie Jerzy became a psychotherapist? Camp Jerzy?

James You never met Jerzy! And camp people can be psychotherapists! –

Hattie Gym bunny, Kylie Minogue, Heaven, Ted Baker shirt, poppers –

James What / the fu—?

Hattie – sculpted eyebrows, Jean Paul Gaultier / aftershave –

James There's no need to be homophobic about / it!

Hattie I'm being nineties about / it.

James – he *was* a fitness – but after I dunno ten years I gently suggested, another string to the bow, Jerzy? and he got *very* cross with me, next thing I know he's enrolled at the

Open University and bish bosh he's a practising Jungian, and if you must know I regret sticking my oar into *his* life, because *our* life became very [stressful] because he was always *probing* into my [unconscious] and obviously I'd spent most of *my* life suppressing all / the

Hattie Yes, I can imagine, / yes,

James so things were *very*

Hattie Yes, / I'm sure,

James and then he *left* me, Jerzy *left* – for a posh cunt named James.

Silence.

Hattie Are you working on something new, James?

James Yes. Yeah, snowed under. And I teach. It's always been peak and trough for me – and societally right now things are [crazy] – it's almost like overnight –

Hattie Don't say all the women are taking your jobs.

James What?

Hattie Don't say all the women are taking your jobs.

James I wasn't going – well, I – no – the point is, th-th-the real structural prejudice against me is how *old* I, I, I *didn't* snitch. To your teacher, I didn't,

Hattie You did,

James No, I remember because my stepmother's never touched a drink in her life – Rosamund is *still* as pure as the driven snow and I –

Stops. She stares.

Hattie Your stepmother? She's still alive?

James Wh-why wouldn't she – I mean, she is old. Dad died. She still lives in the house I grew up in. If you remember that?

Hattie (*shakes head*) I never met her. I only ever saw her across rooms. (*Pause.*) God. The dragon. She must be tough as they come.

James Dragon?

Hattie That's what you used to call her, dragon.

James What? I did not –

Laughter from somewhere: he takes it personally; pours teapot, none left,

– why would you say that, I'm devoted to Rosamund and she to me, I'd die before I called her that – let me get you more – peppermint yeah? – or come on, don't be so Sober Sally, have some of this gorgeous plonk –

Hattie I don't want anything / else –

James – I've just come from reciting Rosamund a poem for God's sake, it's our Saturday morning thing, forty years of endless poetry, very beautiful and depressing this week if the words 'Sylvia' and 'Plath' mean anything to you, Daddy issues, suicide and Nazis, fabulous start to my weekend,

Hattie I don't think I should have agreed to this,

James so um since Jerzy left me, I see quite a lot of Chrissie.

She turns to him: a strange, silent state of their own.

Not physically, obviously, but . . . I thought I was talking to my cat in the kitchen, turns out it's my sister. She's a terrific listener, I suppose not being real helps. She's still a child, seven . . . I think that's why it keeps happening: it's hard to tell a seven-year-old to buzz off, also she's quite bolshie. I keep things light, I don't pretend if she'd lived she'd be, you know, at Number 10, not that on current evidence she'd need to be exceptional for that, I just whinge to her about, well, systemic ageism, but she's very provoking, for example you say you've lost your life to the tax office she says I've lost mine to twentieth-century English homosexual composers,

34

I say, Michael Tippett, Chrissie, Benjamin Britten – I like the American homosexual Aaron Copland *too*, then she laughs and says, are you worried about this new virus in China, I say Bird Flu, Chrissie, Ebola, none of them came here, to *Blackheath* – except they did that's why it's called Blackheath – no, don't look at me like that, I don't, you know, See Dead People, and in fact, I haven't seen her since the morning I was walking on Blackheath . . . and my phone . . . and there you were. (*Pause.*) Playing. Playing again. At last.

Hattie I've often played, I play a lot –

James No – you haven't touched a piano in years, I know that in my gut – not because you played badly, you can't play badly – and you *don't* own a piano, do you, no, you hadn't even told your wife you *could* play, had you? – I knew *that* – I mean I didn't know till today there *was* a wife, or a *daughter* –

Hattie They both know everything now.

She stares. He holds it.

James Every day of my life I've wanted to come to you, Hats. I have this recurring dream, I call and call you, and then that morning *you* were calling *me* –

Hattie It wasn't intentional –

James – you played the public piano at St Pancras railway station like Rachmanifuckingnoff on speed, it wasn't *unintentional*. (*Pause.*) You can't have thought I wouldn't *hear*. (*Pause.*) And I'm happy I did because you and I . . .

Hattie What? You and I what?

James (*entwines fingers*)

Hattie When did Jerzy leave you?

James Twenty-fourth of June 2016.

Hattie When did you meet him?

James Seventeenth of May 1988.

Hattie And in all that time – you're right – I never laid eyes on him. You and I – what, Cathy and Heathcliff? I *didn't* call you . . . I never have . . . not when my daughter was born . . . Mum died . . . (*pushes his wine away pointedly*) when in May I got a new liver. Because you and I . . .

She is still. Foyer hum returns. She texts, then prepares to leave.

James So the sex is off, then? You *have* changed: you used to have a sense of humour.

Hattie And you, James, you entirely lacked one – a shag with you, look at those cords, obviously I'd catch something.

James Gonorrhoea, from me: I wish.

He chuckles, she can't resist, it builds, old friends. He reaches for her hand and it dies.

Why? Why did you play?

Distant, timeless children singing.

Hattie For my sixtieth we had a party, it was lovely, Bo gave the speech. The next day we were off to France, our last trip as Europeans, the first since my operation. Bo's an academic, she's good at speeches. Somehow she put our whole lives into five minutes, and twenty-one years and a daughter *is* a *life*, but . . . all the stuff I'd [suppressed], everything she knew never to ask about, I was so sad so much was missing, and I'm never sad anymore. I wanted to scream: you don't know me, true, I haven't let you, but it's my party and, and – the next day at the station, she was buying coffee and this piano – who puts those things there? – it was just *there* so I . . . walked towards it, and . . .

Echoes of the beguiling piano tune.

Then Bo came back, and of course I was being filmed, all our friends started messaging – and now even you're here because it was *your music* that I played. (*Pause.*) The only thing that came to my fingers was *you*, James.

The music has faded.

James Can I see you again?

Hattie I have to go,

James Please don't, let / me

Hattie *Arbuthnot*! Not *Arkwright*, Mrs Arbuthnot: (*chants*) 'James-James-Where-Is-The-Melody, blahdeddy / blah –'

James James-Hats-Muckers-Forever-Muckers-Forever-Are – (*knocks wine*)

Hattie – oh for fuck's sake, Piggy –

James – sorry – no, not / 'Piggy' –

Hattie – you know, what's funny is we never fucked but it *feels* like we did and not once, over and / over,

James – please, just, when did your mum die, I loved / Mrs B,

Hattie – have you got any weed?

James What?

Hattie Oh forget it, you always were a goody two shoes – who was that footballer on the teacups in *Noye's Fludde*, Charlie somebody? – you wanted him so badly, but you just *didn't have the / balls –*

James Um, mind-blowingly, I do. Have weed.

Hattie On you?

James Yes.

Hattie Can I have it?

James Um. Aren't you an addict?

Hattie Now, motherfucker, before Bo gets back.

James Right. Um. (*Takes paperback out of pocket, bag of weed out of paperback.*)

Hattie Dear God, you have a Penguin paperback in your cardigan pocket, dear God dear God dear God / dear God –

James I'll, I'll get you more – is this to control the pain? – do you want something stronger? –

Hattie I don't have cancer, I just want to / get fucked!

James – I don't know the quality of that because I don't smoke much – but next time skunk, top-quality / skunk –

Hattie *I don't want anything else from / you.*

James I forgive you, Hattie, I FORGIVE YOU.

He is holding her. People are watching. Bo arrives. Hattie doesn't stop looking at him.

Bo Hattie? We can make the twelve forty-one.

James For Chrissie. I forgive you.

Silence.

Hattie I'm relieved you're close to your stepmother. I'm relieved she has you. Goodbye, James.

The children are in uncanny duet with echoes of the beguiling piano music. She leaves. He tries to call, 'Hats! Bo!?' but the music builds, the piano is on the move, and now the music turns into a cinematic orchestral version. It isn't precisely the same as the opening music – not only is it orchestrated, it's less rhythmically and harmonically complex, and entirely major key – but it's the same melody, and more manipulatively lush and beguiling because of a Hollywood sheen. The piano stops downstage of an interior window that divides a warehouse recording studio. On piano: manuscript, a miniature Christmas tree. The orchestra gives way to James playing a Brittenesque song without its words – musically very different from the beguiling tune. After a while he stops, frustrated. He looks at manuscript. Flings it down. Plays. Nokia mobile rings.

James Hello? Hi, I still don't know, give me five minutes. Yeah, I need to decide or she'll put a curse on me because, you know, that's what witches do. I'll ring in a sec.

He hangs up. Groans. Idly plays two notes a semitone apart, oscillating. Hattie appears behind the glass like a ghost. Different clothes, not badly dressed, but somehow dressed too much. Bag. Crappy umbrella. He sees her – gets a fright. She ad-libs ['Sorry, I didn't mean to scare you']. He can't hear her in his sound-proofed room. She realises ['You can't hear?'], gestures ['I'll come in there?'], and pushes the heavy door. Silence.

Hattie I was going to press the buzzer with your name, but some bloke in combats was leaving the building and it's pissing down so I . . . (*Pause.*) Hello.

James (*stares*) How did you find me?

Hattie You found me.

James What? You're wearing two scarves.

Hattie What?

James You're wearing two scarves, are you stoned?

Hattie You're wearing cords from before James Callaghan, maybe I am. (*Pause.*) You look . . . except for the clothes . . . really fit. You do, James, you don't look forty, not at *all*. (*Waits.*) Oh you [flatterer], stop it, don't I?

DECEMBER 1999

Your own studio?

She steps further in. He closes the piano.

James I, I don't own it.

Hattie I used to work not far from here, isn't that mad? I can't tell if it's expensive and cool or cheap and shit?

39

James It's not shit. I get it cheaply. A mate, mates' rates.

Hattie We dreamt of a life like this. (*Pause.*) Are you working on something new? I heard your siren. Is it part of some . . . postmodern . . . atonal . . . something new?

James Oh – no, I'm – remaking – it's a song cycle, the opening's in F-sharp major but the soprano who commissioned it wants it in F, so . . .

Hattie (*pause*) F's easier. But why have no sharps when you can have – (*rusty theory; mnemonic, counts on fingers*) Gay Dave Ate Eleven Bollocks Fried – six.

James (*pause*) Her little demand has consequences for the whole cycle.

Hattie Oh – yeah, / course –

James The um butterfly effect?

Hattie God, absolutely, bloody semitones,

James What are you doing here?

She steps towards him. He is touch-me-not.

Hattie James, I'm dying. (*Tears –*) Cancer. Bones, brains, doctors say I won't make it to the Sydney Olympics and I've trained so hard in synchronised swimming – (*Fake tears.*) Sorry. Just through a shit patch, so just relearning how to take the piss. Plus I'm a bit pissed. Fancy a drink, Bunch of Grapes on the corner, great pub?

James No –

Hattie *You* called *me*.

James I don't know what you / mean by that –

– she takes off layers, puts belongings on piano (which bothers him), rummages in bag: CD, bottles (she swigs intermittently throughout), fags, newspaper article –

Hattie I won't stay – just one quick – I wasn't going to come – obviously we're not *meant* and obviously I've *always* respected, but – (*Stops. Lifts lid.*) A Bechstein. (*Pause.*) Does this belong to your mate?

James Um: yeah: no, it's mine, I – (*closes lid*)

Hattie Someone's loaded.

James – I, I got it cheap, the soundboard's had it and there are more grands than people who want them now,

Hattie It's a beautiful Bechstein grand and it's identical to my mother's.

Drinks. He looks at his watch.

James Please listen,

Hattie (*offers bottle*)

James I'm working,

Hattie Brahms spent his whole life absolutely Liszt.

James That's not true: you must leave. I mean it: you *have* to go.

She presses the newspaper article on him. He glances at it.

Hattie A few weeks ago I hadn't told my girlfriend Jacqui I'd been fired from my job and this was day three of me leaving home pretending to go to work but actually killing time by walking through London like Mrs sodding Dalloway. Jacqui found out and now I've lost my job *and* Jacqui, but they both sucked, especially Jacqui, later we'll have dinner and I'll catch you up on Christ twenty-one years, do you remember when 1999 was just an album by Prince and now our thirties are [kaput]? – how were yours? – and your twenties? – mine? – two decades of civil war among the lesbians and a career in the stimulating world of debt collection. (*Pause.*) London's an utter dump of a city, (*stabs air with index fingers, squashing people*) and by early afternoon I was in a shopping centre in the Swamps of Sadness, aka Surrey Quays, when I was grabbed – not by a man, a force, James, this kind of *Star Wars* Force *pulled* me out of the Sainsbury's white-wine aisle and into a cinema.

Silence. Again he glances at his watch.

James You [have to go] . . . you became a debt collector?

Hattie Debt collection agent. (*Pause.*) I never go to the cinema. I didn't know this film – *Saving Charlotte's* – was successful. I sat down. It started. There was your name. (*Smiles: this is sincere.*) And it was *extraordinary*, James. Not the film so much – that was just Juliet Stevenson gets a brain tumour in Holland Park – but *your music*, the score *you wrote*, on this piano probably, it was, well, it made me happy, happy for you, and for the first time in so long *happy*. (*Stares, smiling. CD.*) I slipped the soundtrack down my top at HMV, I looked you up, (*article*) I read that Q&A, you say there you wrote the music for someone you loved – well, I already knew *that*.

Silence.

James Not you.

Silence.

Hattie God, how mortifying. For you. Obviously I knew you didn't mean me. (*Pause.*) It wasn't hard to find you. You and I are (*entwines fingers*) and I had to come and tell you, because say I didn't, and I, I dunno, died, innocently-naturally died, you wouldn't know, you'd assume teenage-Sylvia-Plath-head-in-the-oven [bleugh], but (*with CD*) it's beautiful, James, beautiful and if if – (*lifts piano main lid, which causes chaos; her things, the Christmas tree, his manuscripts slide off*) if you squished my brain like a peach inside this piano right now I'd die *happy*.

She drops lid, too carelessly for his liking. He clumsily gathers her belongings, holds them towards her. Silence.

James I'm driving to Suffolk. My boyfriend's expecting me. I have to go.

Hattie Boyfriend?

James Yeah.

Hattie Really?

James Why – why the surprise?

Hattie What's his name?

James Jerzy.

Hattie Jersey? Like – potatoes? Like New Jersey, like *The Sopranos*?

James No, J.E.R.Zee.Y.

Hattie Zee?

James He's Polish-American, so probably / zee –

Hattie How long have you been with Jerzee?

James Since, um, 1988.

Hattie Before the Berlin Wall?! Well fucking done, James, what's that in heterosexual years?! What does Jerzy do?

James He's, um, a fitness guy, instructor kind of guy –

Hattie No.

James Yes, at a Topnotch.

Hattie Suffolk? (*Pause.*) I know who had a house in Suffolk. Your homomusical god: Benjamin Britten. (*Pause.*) Do you have a house in Suffolk?

James No, that would be obnoxious. (*Pause.*) We have a house in Blackheath and a sort of shack in Suffolk.

Hattie (*slow nod*) Jerzy must be *very* pleased about the success of your film.

James You know, it *is* successful, but it's not *Four Weddings and a Funeral*.

Hattie No, it wasn't busy when I saw it – maybe three of us? – and this pervert, he sat two seats away when there was a *sea* of empty seats.

James (*pause*) This was in the middle of the day?

Hattie This was on a Thursday afternoon in Surrey Quays, yes.

James Well, an afternoon showing isn't going to be full.

Hattie Not of *Charlotte's Web*, no.

James *Saving Charlotte's* – it's quite a big sleeper / hit.

Hattie Hollywood movie, I / know.

James It's British –

Hattie But produced by that American – sleazy –

James What?

Hattie – that kind of [ugh] producer [fat] he looks like a gangster actually –

James He's not the producer – it's BBC / Films,

Hattie BBC / Films!?

James he's *distributing* it in America and he's not sleazy, he's just meticulous, he knows what he wants.

Hattie What else does your boyfriend do, aside from – ? (*Gestures: pump weights.*)

James What? –

Hattie That's his *whole* / career?

James – don't put that [bottle] on the / piano –

Hattie – no other strings to his / bow?

James – I never put liquids on / the –

Hattie Sorry – fuck, / sorry –

James Hats, *get out* GET OUT.

He throws her belongings at the door. Long silence.

Hattie No one calls me Hats. Just you and Chrissie.

James I didn't. Call you.

She puts the bottle on the piano. Presses a key. Plays second note, a semitone lower, and oscillates, until it falls – now seemingly inevitably, as if this is what had been deferred each time – into the opening figure of Beethoven's 'Für Elise', but she must remove her hand as he closes the lid. She makes to leave. Stops.

Hattie Music is meant to be a consolation. But when she died . . . the exact second that man's van hit my car . . . it's a real thing, this . . . music is . . . abhorrent to me, it's . . . that second, over and over, and if I let music enter me, then my whole . . .

Silence.

So picture me in that cinema. And afterwards – life had been shit – afterwards walking out and finding even Surrey Quays not shit, like I dunno like *I* was in a film, I was Juliet Stevenson with six weeks to live – except I had a lifetime, because it was *music* in my ears again, my oldest, dearest friend's: *yours.*

Silence.

I know you wrote it for her – you basically say it in this article, it's explicit in the music – and because you were *able* to write it, I don't believe you still blame me. You don't, do you, James? The poor Greek bloke was over from Cyprus to see his grandchildren and he turned the wrong way in his son's delivery [van] – I know I wasn't looking where I was – I was upset, shouting, but that man still turned the wrong – you've always known that, you've accepted it, it *wasn't my* [fault] . . .

Nothing.

45

Well. It consoled me. And there's nothing you can do about that because you can't control what people hear in what you write, it's not for you to say how they [feel] . . .

Nothing. She nods, resigned. Pulls heavy door, leaves. Stillness. He opens piano, plays, as if restarting work. But something deeply suppressed erupts in his body: an intense physical reaction. Half-recovers. Plays. The beguiling music, a piano reduction of the orchestral version. She materialises behind the glass, as if she never left. Music builds. She pushes door, enters. She is behind him, close, he knows it. She holds her hand at his back, wanting to touch him, not daring. He stops on an imperfect/interrupted cadence. Silence.

Fuck me.

James ?

Hattie *You?*

James Oh. Yeah. It's a gondola.

Hattie Is it?

James I was in Venice, I was emotional. (*Pause.*) I was twenty-two, it was 1982, I was in love with this Italian called Federico, I'd taken him to all the *Death in Venice* film locations, it wasn't a very successful day, I'd sort of extinguished the fire of our affair –

Hattie Had you really?

James He preferred David Bowie to Thomas Mann and Visconti and Benjamin Britten,

Hattie May I have his phone number?

James so that night I said: let's pretend like in *Death in Venice* there's a deadly plague

Hattie You *kept / going?*

James and it's our last night alive, how much would James drink then, how much *fun would James the Spod be then* and we were staggering home and suddenly, '*Signore*, tattoo?' and I was just *so* sick of everyone thinking I was this shy, suburban – it could be worse!

She laughs, uncontrollably: it couldn't be worse. She tries to say sorry. Silence.

You've changed so much. I didn't recognise you.

Hattie Yes you did. (*Raises bottle.*) To you. And Venice. And poor fucking Federico.

James Federico's *dead*! Well, a *real* plague arrived, didn't it, just for the gays. Yeah: everyone I love or who loves me is dead and everyone else *isn't*!

Hattie Oh diddums, I love you, I do, I always have – oh good, I said in the pub, I'm going to tell him that today,

James You never loved me! (*Takes bottle, swigs.*) Okay, we've had a drink. Go.

Hattie I loved you more than you'll ever know.

James Fuck off, Hattie! Y-you *played* me. You wore me occasionally when you let me visit your house on Saturday mornings, like an accessory, like a – Gauloises cigarette or a CND badge.

Hattie Well, James, the thing is you were such a stuck-up, insufferable, anoraky, pretentious, suburban piggy of a boy – look at you *now*! Still all those things – with a tat! And a composer! and Suffolk! it's sort of adorable, you're almost cool, and so casually homosexual, with a boyfriend, is he real?

James Yes he's / real!

Hattie (*rhythmically plinking bottle, squawking*) 'The coming of the flood . . .'

James The jism of the flood actually, that's what the third-formers used to sing, the jism of the flood,

Hattie Dinner: you're paying: (*with his Nokia*) hello gymnahsium, inform Jerzy weekend sodomy on Aldeburgh Beach is off,

James It is *not* / *off*!

Hattie and you're full of shit: this piano *wasn't* cheap, and you bought it because it reminded you of my mother's. Maybe it *is* Louise's,

James It's not,

Hattie maybe it is,

James It's not,

Hattie you went looking for my mother's / py-ahno,

James Why would I do that, *she* has her pyah – or you – oh, is Mrs B dead?

Hattie (*clapping*) If we say I Believe in Fairies.

James Where is it, what happened?

Hattie God knows, sold.

James What? But she promised that to / *you* –

Hattie Oh don't be so obtuse, I told you, I haven't touched a piano since –

   Stops. Silence.

James But . . . you don't mean . . . you didn't give up *completely*?

Hattie (*gestures a hopeless 'Yes'. Takes in piano, runs a finger along it*) God, remember? (*Poses against it provocatively.*) Remember zis? Remember how feminist I was, Clara Schumann never her husband, Delia Derbyshire never Dvořák – (*sees manuscript*) ooooh, your song cycle, the contentious key!

James F-sharp major's not / contentious –

Hattie (*plays chords*) I'm with the soprano, too many sharps, you're dick-waving.

James It's not about my sharps, it's about her shrinking range!

Hattie Oh. Then why shame her? Collaborate, make the dress fit the woman.

Sight reading, she plays a phrase from the vocal line. He watches nervously. She plays the phrase again, now in the lower key. She plays the (rippling, complex) treble accompaniment to the vocal line (in the new key). He approaches uncertainly.

James You really never . . . [play]? . . . You're transposing that at sight, Hattie . . . What about your girlfriend . . . she knows?

Hattie That I was a teenage musical prodigy? No. Nor Suze before Jacqui, Liz before Suze, I could go all the way back to Eve. Eve knew, obviously. You remember Eve.

James Who's Eve?

Hattie Eve. She was my Venice.

She has the feel of the treble accompaniment and la-las the vocal. He sits beside her. He plays the bass. Tentative at first. A fluent, moving duet (wordless) develops. Slowing the tempo to accommodate not the musical challenge but the feelings, she sings the climactic words: 'But nothing drear can move me: / I will not, cannot go'. Silence.

You play fantastic.

James No. I was never a patch on you.

Hattie I suppose some things flow across our synapses forever. (*Leaves piano, drinks.*) Don't look so sad. You got lucky, I lost it, doesn't matter, happens all the time.

James No . . . that's not actually . . . after Chrissie, I, I lost it, I didn't do what I was meant to, for years, I bummed around, tried all kinds / of –

Hattie You went to the Royal College of Music?

James No, of course I didn't, / Hats!

Hattie Okay, okay – how would I / know?

James I floundered, I was a mess –

Hattie Well you found it again. Look at you. That's why I'm here, because I *heard.* (*Pause.*) Now tell me all about Federico, it all sounds so romantic-slash-sad.

James That was a lifetime ago –

Hattie New Jerzy Potato, then, what does the Twink wanna be when he grows up?

James Jerzy is / thirty-three!

Hattie You wanted *us* to shack-up together once, remember?

James Yeah, I wish we had –

Hattie Some grotty bedsit, candle in a Mateus Rosé bottle, yoghurt pots for / glasses –

James I miss the / seventies! –

Hattie (*chants*) James-James-Where-Is-The-Melody
    Benjamin Britt for he,
    Hats-Hats something –
    Fanny Mendelssohn for she!

Both (*not recalling it all*) James Hats friends forever,
    Muckers forever are we,
    If you wanna go down on Hats/James you clown
    FUCK OFF COS S/HE'S WITH –

    – their faces are very close. Silence. Mobile rings. She finds cigarettes.

James Hello? God, sorry, yeah I, (*looks at Hattie*) I've decided to do it, we'll start in F. Yep, the whole cycle modulates. Yes, please. Thanks, Melanie, bye.

Hattie There. The sweet, polite James I remember. And a happy soprano.

James That was my assistant. The witch can stew for the weekend.

Hattie Assistant?

James Student, pianist at Guildhall, I'll lose her when she has a career, which she won't, she's not Fanny fucking Mendelssohn.

She stares. He holds it, just.

You can't smoke in here.

Hattie (*plays right-hand snatches of his beguiling melody*) Did you think I was dead?

James No. Sometimes.

Hattie Same. When I saw your name on *Charlotte's Web* –

James *Saving Charlotte's* –

Hattie I realised how often I'd thought it. So often I'd worried that – well, you'd gone the way of your Italian. And worse – that you'd taken a woman with you. (*Stops playing.*) Remember Cameron Tyler?

James What? Charlie – Charlie / Tyler –

Hattie I remember sitting in the audience for *Noye's Fludde* with my parents – they were still furious I'd been fired after you told Mrs Arbuthnot about my vodka –

James What? No – I didn't – I tried to take the blame / for that –

Hattie – and your dad and Chrissie's mum were a few rows in front – I never met the dragon properly, it was like, I dunno, you blamed her for your Mum's cancer or something – and I was watching you and Arbuthnot playing, and Chrissie, bless her, was she the Raven or Dove or – but

51

the most mesmerising thing was you, gazing over the piano at Charlie Tyler banging his teacups wishing *you* were a teacup, so over the years I've worried about the consequences of such a stupid secret: what if the dumb boy's still closeted and he's married some girl and gets HIV and kills himself and her – so it's a relief to find you all grown-up with a gym bunny in East Anglia.

James Right. Well. Astounding homophobia, Hattie –

Hattie I'm remembering *your* internalised / homophobia.

James – and I've never been with a woman, or in the / closet –

Hattie How do you know that about your assistant? That she won't have a career?

James Because I've heard her! Melanie doesn't play the piano, she rapes it!

Hattie What a disgusting thing to say.

James I – I – *you* –

Hattie (*plays beguiling melody, both hands*) Have you missed me? I've missed you.

James Do you know what: I haven't.

Hattie This Bechstein suggests otherwise.

James It's not your mum's! I remember every inch of hers, I remember the fucking serial number: nine-four-eight-four-two!

> *She stops. He suddenly swears, makes a call. During it she finds herself playing: Fanny Mendelssohn's Mélodie op. 4, no. 2, which she played several bars of in 1976. Tentative, soon fluent. The music is beautiful – tender and yearning.*

Melanie, hi, I've changed my mind, I'm sticking to F-sharp major. Yeah, she'll have a fit, she's a total hysteric, but it's what I wrote. Okay. Yes, come by on Monday around two, please. (*Melanie has asked what the music is; looks to Hattie.*) I've no idea what it is, something – Romantic. Okay, bye. (*Hangs up. Doesn't know what to do.*)

Hattie What do you think this is about? I think lost love. Like yours and Federico's. Or mine and Eve's. Or *ours* – we could have gone to Venice. I never made it there.

James (*noise!*) I'm sure you've been everywhere.

Hattie Hastings, once.

James Yeah, this is what I remember most about you, Hattie. How full of shit you are. You have no idea how bloody privileged – you had everything handed – and clearly this is all bullshit – you always lied about everything – you still play, on the grand piano you grew up with in your parents' house, or on the *other* one in what you once called their 'shack' in France, we went there, it was no *shack*, so you've been to *France*.

Hattie Seventy-seven, summer of our lives, *c'était l'été de nos vies*, like a French film.

James Not really. *Jules and Jim* maybe where two of them die when she *drives them off a fucking bridge* –

Behind the glass, as Hattie stops, a woman appears like a ghost. She has a suitcase, umbrella and bag of groceries. James freezes.

Rosamund. (*Sotto.*) It's Rosamund.

She doesn't know who he means – back to glass, terrified, he mouths ['Rosamund'] *and tightly gestures* ['Don't move'] *– she remains confused –*

Rosamund, I'll, um –

– and though he tries to stop her, Rosamund enters, carrying all her things, chatting.

Rosamund – we don't want to be late, and the traffic will be awful.

James Hi, / um –

Rosamund I rang the buzzer, a woman was leaving, / so –

James Sorry, I was recording, um, let's . . .

Rosamund (*stares at Hattie. At one point she notices the bottle and mess*)

Hattie Hello.

  Silence.

Rosamund Melanie?

James No, um . . . Melanie's twenty, um . . . Rosamund, it's . . .

Hattie Charlotte, James's lawyer. There's something he needs to sign before the weekend, a contractual thing to do with a soprano.

Rosamund Charlotte?

Hattie Yes.

Rosamund Like James's film?

Hattie Yes. We joke about it. I don't have a brain tumour though.

Rosamund (*pause*) What's Juliet done now?

Hattie Well, you know Juliet Stevenson.

James Juliet McGregor-Smith: the soprano.

Hattie Yes: *McGregor-Smith* Juliet, total hysteric, but that's what they call meticulous women.

Rosamund (*pause*) I'm Rosamund.

James Um – my stepmother –

Hattie Hi.

Rosamund (*pause; re: shopping*) I've brought the talking poem you gave me to listen to on the way, and dinner.

James Oh, y-you didn't need to do that –

Rosamund Jerzy won't have anything in, all he'll have there is protein shakes.

Hattie That's right and maybe steroids! (*Pause.*) I've never met Jerzy, his reputation [precedes him] – where is Jerzy?

Rosamund The Suffolk house.

Hattie makes a knowing noise; James is desperate to get Rosamund out.

James Let's –

Rosamund I heard you playing, Charlotte?

Hattie Me? – no – a bit – it helps to be musical at a classical music agency. I scraped through Grade Three back in the summer of sixty-something, I had this teacher called Madame Schultz but – (*Gestures: she snuffed it.*)

Complex silence: James and Rosamund are confused by different things.

James Madame Schultz?

Rosamund You work at James's *agency*?

Hattie In-house lawyer,

James I'll just see to this – go to the foyer – I won't be – actually, why don't you go to the car? Here –

– he presses keys on Rosamund; she ad-libs ['It's already ten past four – how long? – which floor?']; he likewise ['Near the Barbican – five minutes – leave all that, I'll bring it – second floor, right near the lift, I mean left of the lift']; before he manages to usher her out, she stops and stares at Hattie for a long time.

Hattie Nice to meet you.

They leave. She is stock-still. An impossibly long pause. He returns. All her restraint gives way. She becomes deeply distressed.

55

Why didn't you say she / was [coming] –

James I tried, / I *told* –

Hattie Are we being recorded?

James No, I just said / that –

Hattie (*collects things*) I absolutely would have [left] – did she recognise me? – I only saw her once, at *Noye's* – and at the inquest, she stared at me, she *stared*, James,

James You have to wait / now –

Hattie I *wanted* to meet her but they wouldn't / let me,

James – I can't risk you bumping / into her –

Hattie Because she still blames / me?

James Hattie, / please –

Hattie *Which way do I go?*

They are close, as if locked together, but not touching.

James I have to go. You'll have to let yourself out.

Hattie James, James . . . James, are you happy your music made me happy?

James Actually, leave now: go left: don't go near the / Barbican –

Hattie Are you?

James I try not to care what people think –

Hattie It's not about what people *think* – FEEL! You can't have thought . . . all these years . . . everything you've done . . . City warehouse, sopranos, BBC, you can't have thought I wouldn't, *ever*, *hear*? –

Mobile rings – she finds the humour in it:

– oh and it's motherfucking Melanie again – *oh*! Melanie *lurves* James!

James Hello? Hi. Yeah, we're about to leave. No don't worry she's bringing dinner.

Hattie (*mouths during this: 'Jerzy?'*)

James I don't know, um –

Hattie (*at shopping*) Chicken, that won't last all the way down the / A12 –

James No one –

Hattie (*with tub*) Marinade, home-made! (*Talking book.*) *Goblin Market*: my favourite,

James – just – someone I used to know.

Hattie SOMEONE HE USED TO KNOW.

James (*hangs up, grabs her*) Left, left, go FUCKING LEFT.

Violent. He lets go. Silence.

Hattie Do you know why counselling never did much for me? Because I already knew how to get better. I kept saying: can't I see Chrissie's parents, but they'd decided apparently I wasn't allowed, so I stopped asking. Then life . . . Till one day in Surrey Quays I . . . So before I go . . . please let me hear it as words: you don't blame me. (*Pause.*) I'd kill myself before I hurt that poor woman –

James Hats, Hats, she's all right, I promise, Hats. I don't think she recognised you and even if she did her life is good, she devotes every hour to helping other people, and she doesn't blame anyone, I promise.

Hattie And you?

He can't. She tries to stop her tears.

. . . was Chrissie the Raven . . . or the Dove . . . I can't [remember] . . .

He gently hushes her, moves close. No touch. They stand for ages. She nods, picks up the last of her things, wipes face. She's ready. Too many clothes and things, but ready.

We're so old.

James It's the end of the century, Hats. We're ancient.

She reaches for his hand. Nothing. A moment. She da-das some Britpop song. Sweet, slow. Dances a bit. A few mangled lyrics. For herself, her own world – drunk, but not silly. He watches. It builds. It becomes disturbing – and segues into strident la-la-ing of his beguiling melody. Goes wildly off key. Her moves goad him. Stops, close to him.

Hattie So enjoy Suffolk, and farewell. (*Courtier's bow, snorts.*) Suffolk. It is a homo-composer thing, isn't it? What's after *Charlotte's Tumour* and the song cycle, an opera for boys in your little pink house by the sea? (*Sings mockingly.*) 'Peter Grimes!' (*Pause.*) 'Peter Grimes!'

James Of course you were taking the piss the whole time.

Hattie Why would you think that?

James I'm just doing my thing, Hattie.

Hattie Your 'thing'?

James I'm sorry things haven't worked out for you.

Hattie And as I've said over and over I'm happy they have for / *you* –

James YOU'RE WRONG, ALL RIGHT? What you heard has nothing to do with Chrissie or you. I wrote that music for my boyfriend whom you'll *never* know, nothing in my work has anything to do with *you*. It made you happy, I'm happy, but I have to go to my family now.

Opens door. She passes him.

And it's called *Saving Charlotte's* and it's a sweet film about love.

Hattie (*stares*) Oh. (*Chuckles.*) You think it's *good*. Jamie. Juliet Stevenson sacrifices the last six weeks of her life so she can save and give her ballet school to Jonathan Pryce? And

58

since we're talking about your 'thing', the truth is I didn't like that either. It *didn't* console me. It was like listening to nuclear fallout. Dead on arrival. An unsurprising wedding cake: layer after layer of diminishing layers.

James Well, it bought me the big blue house by the sea.

Hattie Oh, *that* justifies it being about a blow-up doll of a woman, written by a bloke, directed by a bloke, with a bloke to whom the woman has to account in every scene: it's a man's requiem for – not a *real* / woman –

James All this? Not my problem.

Hattie This?

James The scarves, booze, you stink – and you were always jealous of me.

Hattie All I am is sad.

James Pull the door shut behind you, debt collector.

Hattie There's the James I remember.

James You always were a fucking bitch.

Hattie Ah, *there* he is.

   She pours vodka into the piano. Silence.

Don't overreact. I'll pay. Could I have your assistant's job so I can pay?

   They are very upset.

Just acknowledge it. What are we if you won't? I'm your *oldest / dearest* –

James Then why did you leave me, Hattie? You didn't love me. You despised me because you were jealous –

Hattie I loved you –

James No – *you* were dead on arrival, you didn't have what it took to be Kate fucking Bush let alone – you couldn't stand I was more talented and *you left me.*

Perversely, she smiles. 'Kate Bush' has prompted it.

He turned the wrong way, but you were hysterical and probably drunk –

Hattie But that's a lie, isn't it, and if I was hysterical so were you –

James I never want to see you / again –

Hattie (*a kind of ecstasy grows*) James, James, remember? No. Because you couldn't. You're a girl on the cusp of life, James. Everything's been parents and Bach and a piano teacher who hates everything you bring him, and then you watch *Top of the Pops* and you see something that makes you go, there, *there it all is*, and you meet someone and they say, I love what you're doing and thinking, and they give you books and records – and you think that was *you*, you *dumb prick*? Jealous of you – of what, mate, of *this*?! I couldn't have understood a thing about anything then, and yet I and Eve and even my mother, Mrs Arbuthnot, my first piano teacher, *all the women*, they all understood everything more than any *man* or *you* – and until you turned up with your sister that Saturday I was so close to changing my life, James, I *was so close*. (*Hands to face. Pulls herself together.*) Can I stay in Blackheath for a few nights while you're away? (*Pause.*) Have you got a tenner? (*Pause.*) It's the best film score since *Taxi Driver*, have you got five quid?

James (*makes to leave*)

Hattie Don't go, you've more to say . . . I wish you *had* been recording because then you could rewind and it'd prove I've given you chances to say it: I wrote that music.

James (*stops*)

Hattie I wrote it.

Echoes of the beguiling music – perhaps.

James What? That's a lie.

Hattie Well, there's no proof. I used to record myself, Mum threw away all my tapes and manuscripts, sold my sheet music, piano, I *made* her get rid of everything, I was *relieved* to see everything *gone*.

James (*pause*) Pull the door shut behind you.

Hattie Oh yes, I mind. If that's what you're asking me. I *mind*. I *mind terribly*. (*Pause.*) But what's talent? Talent's cheap. And it *must* mean you forgive me. (*Pause.*) Then again, when you think about it, it's *I* who has to forgive *you*. Because when you think about it, James Culler – Music by James Culler – you *always got everything you wanted*,

James What I wanted? I lost that woman's daughter. My sister. You aren't meant to come back.

He leaves. Alone in safety light and silence, she stares at the piano. Slowly, she drops a finger towards a key, and as it hits, the Britpop song – 'Disco 2000', say – plays loudly into the interval.

Act Two

In a room with a view to a rainy street, Hattie is staring at an envelope. Elsewhere, James – cardigan, raincoat, satchel – is doing the same thing. They open their envelopes and read the letters. She is stock-still. He allows himself to smile.

1978

She rips her letter in half, then in pieces, buries the fragments inside the piano stool, and sits upon it, hard. She puts her hands to her face. He puts his letter back in its envelope, takes a paperback from his cardigan pocket, slips it inside the paperback, and returns paperback to pocket. Rosamund enters.

James No, Rosamund. I'm not speaking to anyone till I've spoken to Hattie.

Rosamund I understand, yes.

She leaves him, and, in shadow outside the door, becomes Hattie's mother.

Louise Hattie?!

Hattie (*looks to door*)

Louise Is that what I think it is?

Hattie No, Mum!

She stands, back to the door, and pulls herself together. She turns to the door – and as Louise disappears James is there, wiping his wet glasses.

Ta-dah!

James (*glasses on*) Oh my – wow.

DECEMBER 1976 – A SATURDAY AFTER *NOYE'S FLUDDE*

Hattie It's a piano not the Second Coming. Unless you're coming? (*Climbs on piano, poses provocatively.*) I give you: Reclining Venus, or whichever-sixteen-year-old-naked-female-of-antiquity-from-the-male-perspective-that-you-prefer.

James Um – sh-should you be doing that?

Hattie Why not?

James Because it's a B-Bechstein –

Hattie And I love zis this Bechstein, je déteste zis Bechstein, oui, non, / oui,

James – it's old – or maybe not so old? turn-of-the-century? does your mum know, where did she get it?

Hattie From *her* mum.

James – can I see the serial number?

Hattie (*strikes note to shut him up*)

James – oh God, it's very out of tune, should I tell her?

Hattie James, how do you get through the day? Perfect pitch must be like having furious little men in your ears listening out for reasons to take offence.

James Yes: it's a gift and a curse.

Hattie (*laughs at his pomposity; flourishes manuscript*) Piece I'm working on. Royal College of Music entrance sample clang clang. A *ballade*, basically my opus one number one: A-major: ugh: it'll modulate. I'd love you to hear it actually – when it's ready – come round again? – now you know the way on the bus?

James Um – (*Nods, thrilled.*) Love your house. Love your mum.

Hattie And *Louise* loves – (*Vodka from piano, swigs. Offers.*) She says Brahms spent his whole life absolutely Liszt.

James Is that true? I don't think / that's –

Hattie She has speed too, darling little blues.

James Oh, um – I'm not really a speed sort of – (*picks up old – precious – sheet music*)

Hattie Protect with your life, it's my Fanny.

James What? Oh.

Hattie I'm addicted to Fanny. Adore her. (*At music with him.*) *Wanderlied*: how sexy are these sextuplets? Honestly, it's so good. It's like some liberating naked spree through the woods. It's like scaling a Bavarian mountain on these blues,

James It-it looks quite pretty.

Hattie *Pretty?* It's spectacular – see? – E-major to G-major to B-flat major to C-sharp minor back to E, / a rising third each time –

James – a rising third – yes, that's / correct.

Hattie – she's wandering the world till she reaches her her her – *Italy*. Which is *home*: she has her feet in Italy the whole time!

James I-I-I you're amazing but I don't think that's how music works actually.

Hattie ?

James It's not *about* things. It's not programmatic, it's absolute.

Hattie So Benjamin Britten's *Sea Interludes* aren't about the North Sea?

James That's different. I'm not really into music before –

Hattie Don't Speak Let Me Guess: *The Young Person's Guide to the* Motherfucking *Orchestra*.

James 1880. Except Bach. I don't like any German Romantic, really. Even though I am quite romantic, I think.

Hattie (*flirtatious*) Are you? We leave tomorrow for our French shack. In summer you can come. We'll smoke Gauloises. Read Rimbaud. Sip Pernod. Eat oysters – and snails.

Their faces are very close.

James It-it-it was sad Britten died, wasn't it? And just before *Noye's Fludde.*

Hattie James. Your little sister with the olive branch in her mouth was the sweetest thing since baby Jesus,

James *Half-* / sister –

Hattie but I had to sit there watching Miss Simpson singing like a mule and cuntry organist Arbuthnot (*piano playing: fists*) demolishing *my* part, yet I still found the strength to find you afterwards and shyly ask for your number, and now you're here I'm starting to wonder: does he even fancy a shag? Or is he terrified of Fanny?

James What? Oh. (*Removes raincoat.*) I hope you can take my tempo.

Hattie Oh, oh, *oh gauntlet*! – (*rushes to piano*) new cords?

James Um, yeah, the Dragon bought them for me: are they all right?

Hattie No: yet for you: *yes* (*counting them in, presto*) One, two, WAIT! – (*makes him stand, gets tape recorder from stool*) let's record this to prove who's the greater talent –

James What, no, put that away –

Hattie – chicken! fine! – (*stands on stool*) ladies and men. Welcome – on this hot summer evening of the future in post-apocalyptic 1989 – to the Wigmore no the Festival no the Royal Goddamn Albert. Before Leonard Bernstein conducts the orchestral suite from my Oscar-winning score to the film of Christina Rossetti's *Goblin Market*, a never-to-be-heard-again performance with a man – it's not his fault and he plays fantastic, I quote his sister Chrissie the Prime Minister,

James Chrissie'll only be – twenty in / 1989! –

Hattie Yes, it's the famous concert pianist, James-James-Where-Is-The-Melody,

James (*improvises short heraldic motif on piano*)

Hattie That cords-from-Marks-and-Spencer-wearing trendsetter, (*sits, improvises 1970s television-jingle-like answer*) that North Sea-loving sailor boy,

James (*improvises* Peter Grimes-*like answer*)

Hattie My fellow traveller, (*improvises Romantic answer*) my secret lover,

James (*stumped by this*)

Hattie My oldest, dearest,

   Time stops.

Let's do this every Saturday.

   Silence.

Fanny Mendelssohn's –

James (*checking*) Opus eight, number / four –

Hattie STEP ON IT, PIGGY.

   They play with terrific skill and feeling. She takes the rippling sextuplets, he the right-hand melody. It's lovely, yearning music. The seasons change,

   1976–1978 – MOST SATURDAYS,
   AND SUMMER 1977 IN FRANCE,

as the music continues,

   UNTIL CHRISSIE'S DEATH

and he leaves the piano as she continues solo, and a table appears, at which he sits

   WELCOME TO THE ROYAL FESTIVAL HALL
   11 APRIL 2024   16.47

and she stops playing but remains at piano, in the depths of the public foyer: the hum of children's voices, and, occasionally, their distant, timeless singing. James nurses wine. Checks his phone. Eventually, Bo arrives.

Bo James?

James Yes? Oh. Hi.

Bo Hi. Yvonne, Hattie's wife. Bo.

James Yes. I remember.

Bo Is that wine?

James Yes, I was – (*stops. Downs it*)

Bo Hattie can't meet you. She sends her apologies.

James (*stares*) I texted an hour ago. I suggested here.

Bo She's performing in a few hours.

James I know, I have a ticket, row C. When we emailed she said saying hello would be okay.

Bo That was a mistake. She forgot about a pre-show TikTok thing. She hasn't even finalised her songlist.

James If it wasn't okay, maybe she shouldn't have got my hopes – Christ, I sound like a [fucking] groupie. (*Pause.*) We met here, didn't we? A whole pandemic ago.

Bo Yes, the day you offered wine to an alcoholic. Then gave her drugs. Shit ones. Bye.

James Bo – um – wait – I, I need to tell Hattie my stepmother died. (*Pause.*) It's okay, she had a good life. Well, a hard life . . . but somehow she [ploughed on]. She was a remarkable person, really. She got an MBE. I'd like to tell Hattie. (*Pause.*) I don't know what you know –

Bo I know everything.

James Gosh. Omniscient Bo. (*Genuflects.*) Okay, so – you're gatekeeper – again – I suppose to be fair she actually needs

67

one this time – with Covid, Rosamund, I've only just sort of come up for air and noticed how famous she's become.

Bo She's not famous.

James No, it wasn't hard to get row C.

Bo It's a festival, she has a following,

James Thousands of followers, I love her songs, the YouTubes I've seen, all from a Psychotic Episode at a train station in rush hour. (*Regrets this.*) She deserves everything good that comes to her, Bo.

Bo Especially after everything you did.

James Okay, fine, I'm no one, I'll post a comment on her TikTok Instagram *fuck*.

   Silence.

Bo You're right. It is arrogant and stupid to say I know everything. I don't . . . and that's part of it, that's part of the love. I don't know what she dreams about. What she was like when she was six. What she ticks at the ballot box,

James Labour. Despite her upbringing.

Bo Really? I don't think so, despite her lyrics. My sister died in the first wave, we don't talk about it because the pandemic helped Hattie – yes, on the back of St Pancras she got a keyboard, wrote songs, uploaded herself – but more than that, I think she thinks that government did a good job. Her right. And the perfectly normal unknowability I'm talking about. It turns me on: a lesbian Tory, you're told they exist, but forty years of post-structural-post-colonial-psychoanalytic-feminist-queer theory at several prestigious universities, I've never actually met one.

   She eats a mint. She offers him one, he wants it, she withdraws the offer.

'Psychotic episode'. Honestly.

68

James Well, wasn't it? When you came back from Costa Coffee or wherever and saw her playing like that you must have thought she'd lost her bloody marbles, or you had.

Bo No. Oh, I was shocked. The sight of her, her ability. But it was *music* . . . so it had to be an expression of some . . . deep love, and what I thought was: she's met someone. She's leaving me for Beyoncé or the CEO of Médecins Sans Frontières. (*Pause.*) I got you. So that was an enormous relief. (*Eats another mint. Silence.*) I'd never seen this film. *Saving Charlotte's*. Sweet Jesus.

James I suppose it's a bit of a relic now –

Bo I wondered if I'd got to it in the Tardis.

James The nineties are a long time ago –

Bo Produced by the famous Hollywood rapist.

James He wasn't the *producer*, he was the / *distributor* –

Bo A pre-9/11 London, oblivious fairyland filled with blue doors and independent bookshops – well, I suppose Bosnia *was* a long way away –

James It was made three years after Bosnia and what is wrong with the world, not every story can tell every story!

Bo And only white people in Holland Park.

James I didn't cast it, I just wrote the score!

She stares. He can't hold it.

Bo To have lost a little girl in an accident like that, and so to lose, of all things, music. When I understood that's what had happened, that she'd ripped it out of herself like / that –

James But she's found it again – look at her – she has it back –

Bo And I'm still not used to it, James. *My* world turned upside down too. And *I* caused it: my birthday speech, all those secrets I didn't know, or need to know, which led to St Pancras. Now tell me: *at* St Pancras, why would she play music apparently written by you twenty years *after* you were friends? – why would her brain take her to something the two of you *didn't* share? So you see, I believed her on the train to France when she told me *she* wrote what she played, and now your stepmother's died and Hattie no longer has to live with the terror of compounding that poor woman's suffering, perhaps she'll finally *hang you out to dry* –

James Please, it's why I'm here, I'm clearing out Rosamund's and I found something and-and-and if she's a stranger to you, Bo, that's not my fucking fault!

Children's screams: play, but mistaken by him, at first, as distress.

Bo Do you know what I think? I think you've lived your whole life humming with a kind of hatred for us. For women.

James What? That's / ridiculous –

Bo It's a soft hum. Level two, not ten. You've got away with it, because most people thought, if they thought at all, level two's not bad, it's not as loud as most men's, and he's gay, so he has his own Gay Things to deal with, so it'd be mean to call him out on it. Let's substitute, I don't know, homophobia for your soft-hum misogyny –

James I'm / not misog—

Bo – I mean your *own* homophobia, the kind I bet you had at one point when you were young, like lots of us in the sixties and seventies, you turned *that* off, yes? One day you said, to hell with this, I'm not going to hate myself for this, this is who I am – I've just stumbled on Byron or a novel by James Baldwin or E. M. Forster, I've just discovered Tchaikovsky or the Village People or Benjamin Britten, I'm on the same path as millions of men throughout history just like me – fabulous, we're here, we're queer: so why couldn't you turn off your envy and fear of women? Let's substitute racism – any ism you can think of – yes, it's an old song, humming away, not so most people would hear, just *there*.

70

Sounds and gestures a soft pulse. Silence. She has another mint.

James People aren't all good or bad . . . and if it gives you satisfaction, I'm relieved Covid was the making of her because everything went tits up here, I couldn't teach down bloody Zoom, I got angry, haemorrhaged students, I sold my Blackheath house – please may I have a mint?

For the rest of the scene, Hattie plays fragments.

Bo I knew the day I met her she had history, James. She'd been to a job interview drunk, I bought a beef sandwich for a suicidal addict, I *knew*.

James Chicken. Chicken not beef. Then you went to a church. St Mary-le-Bow.

Bo Beef. And the church was St Clement's.

James St Mary-le-Bow, that's why you're called Bo, Bo.

Bo Except it was St Clement's – and do call me Yvonne – it took me twenty-one years to correct Hattie because it only would have reminded her, and revealed to our daughter Frances, what a drunken mess she was.

James Right, see, the *past* is a mess, maybe *you're* wrong and *I'm* / right!

Bo Maybe you'd like to read my book *Gothic Slave Narratives*, Oxford University Press 2003, I was researching it in the City that day, the Shelleys got married in a church on Cannon Street destroyed by Hitler, so I know which surviving churches I went into, and after I bought Hattie the beef sandwich, we went to St Clement's.

James Which she left because the organist was playing Mendelssohn.

Bo No, it was a carol, it was close to Christmas.

James Yes, Yvonne, that's Mendelssohn, that's 'Hark! The Herald / Angels –'

Bo After St Clement's I grabbed her by one of the two scarves she was wearing, pulled us into a cab, took her home and we had frenzied sex like a pair of insatiable Bacchae.

James (*stares*) Two scarves . . . ?

Bo I'm very sorry about your sister. And about her mother.

James (*taking package from satchel*) Wait, no, please, Rosamund's was my childhood home, and when I was clearing things out, I found this old cassette in an old cardigan of mine, it'd been rotting at the back of my old bedroom wardrobe for forty years – but it still plays. I've put it in a Walkman so she can listen – and also, Bo, I've been searching for her mother's piano, I contacted every dealer in – I tracked it down to this evil old cunt in Bristol, he refused to sell, / but –

Bo Go home.

James no, I'm watching her tonight – wait! (*Makes her take package.*) Tell her to listen. I'll email now explaining everything, I'll wait by the stage door – / Bo?!

Hattie appears to be playing as Bo leaves, but it is in fact Kate Bush's 'Oh to Be in Love'. The song grows, the piano is on the move, and James disappears as it stops in the room with a window to a rainy street, where, with the LP cover (The Kick Inside), *Hattie is digging the song: teenage ecstasy. On piano: record player from which the song blares, candle in a Mateus Rosé bottle. Inspired, she puts the cover on a pile of sheet music and writes feverishly on manuscript. She turns the song off and removes from the stool the tape recorder, inserts tape, hits record, eats yoghurt, plays the oscillating semitones. Doorbell. She is surprised. Looks at her watch. Swears. Wonders what to do. Climbs on piano, poses provocatively. Enter James – cardigan, raincoat, satchel, wiping his glasses.*

Hattie I give you: Dido, Pining for Aeneas.

James Get off please. Honestly, this family, you all treat the family silver like dirt.

1978 – A SATURDAY –
THE MORNING AFTER THEIR LETTERS

Sorry, I'm moist: Chrissie's fault, she left our umbrella on the bus.

Hattie You need to get your driving licence, man – and a car!

James We can't all afford a c-car, *man* –

Hattie Why have you brought Chrissie?

James Don't ask. I left her with your mum, they're making fairy cakes.

Hattie Did *Mum* let you in, or – ?

James Your dad's playing golf. Has she just got up? It's ten thirty. I love Mrs B.

Hattie You think Louise is a malignant narcissist who plays this piano like a bitch.

James I do not think your mother's a malignant narcissist. Though she was a bit – were you out last night? – I rang – it was after nine – she was slightly –

Hattie Off her fucking face?

James Have *you* just got up?

Hattie I've been working my tits off in here since six thank you.

James Oh! (*Removes raincoat.*) Are you working on something new?

Hattie Remaking something old. How are you, James? You look well.

James Do I? I am well, actually. I'm cool actually –

73

Hattie (*laughs: he's not cool*)

James – how are *you*, Hats?

Hattie Post-coital. Knackered.

James Oh. Is the sex off, then?

Hattie Not if it's my turn.

James Yeah, we played Michael Tippett last week.

Hattie That sonata was *music*?

James Shut up.

Hattie Lili Boulanger or Clara Schumann?

James Makes no difference.

She glances at him. Searches through sheet music. He watches. Silence.

Hattie Is that Old Spice?

James Um . . . Brut 33. (*Silence. Sniffs.*) Are *you* wearing new perfume?

Hattie Gauloises, Pernod and sweat.

He stares. She searches. Silence. He has paperbacks in both cardigan pockets. He starts to take one out –

James I . . . I . . . (*but he changes his mind. He produces a paperback from the other cardigan pocket*) I read your *Bell Jar*.

Hattie Did you *die*?

James It is quite depressing so I'm reading *A Clockwork Orange*.

Hattie Oh, that one with the guy who loves Beethoven and he rapes two girls while listening to the Ninth Symphony?

James Yeah and then they cure him of violence with behaviour modification and he loses his musicality which is *really* disturbing.

74

Hattie Yeah but he stops raping people! – (*sees LP cover, thrusts it at him*) oh my God you *have* to listen to the last song on side one!

James (*reads*) 'Wuthering Heights'? –

Hattie You must've heard it, it's on Radio One non-stop – oh: so you haven't – did you see her on *Top of the Pops*?! –

James Song called 'Wuthering Heights', (*eats her yoghurt*) bit pretentious.

Hattie Oh how delicious, I just got that on tape.

James What?

Hattie (*with tape recorder*) It's recording – I told you, I'm / working –

James No no tape over that, I can't stand the sound of my / voice! –

Hattie (*climbs on piano with recorder*) And delete your penetrating analysis of the great works of the Second Sex? Never! '*The Bell Jar*? Quite depressing. "Wuthering Heights"? Bit pretentious' –

James Hattie –

Hattie – future historians will find this cassette, and have a window into our middle-class adolescent des-o-lation. (*Poses.*) I give you: Ophelia in the Suburbs. Mermaid-like, drenched in her piano partner's cologne – Suffolk Breeze, by James – she chanted old songs by neglected lady composers, till her bell-bottoms, heavy with their boredom, blah-blah-blah-blah, teenage death. (*Dies.*) You've got a stiffie.

James I have not!

Hattie (*leaps off*) God, aren't you just *dying* to leave school, I'm so ready to *plunge*!

James Yes! – on Wednesday Mr Simpson and I had quite a good conversation about the Balinese influences in *Death* *in Venice* and today I think I'm just so beyond Mr Simpson now, you know?!

They stare. Silence.

Hattie Fuck shagging. Let's lick the bowl before Chrissie gets it all – or maybe Eve's up and Eve's licking it, you can meet Eve –

James (*erupts*) No I'm sick of Chrissie, I never asked for Chrissie, Dad's always fishing and the Dragon's started reading for the blind and I always have to babysit, it's not fair, Rosamund knows Saturdays are the one day I get to see you! Who's Eve?

Hattie Are you seriously telling me your stepmother reads for the blind? – is there *no end to that woman's cruelty*?! (*Marches out.*)

James Hattie, Hats, speaking of plunging, should we move in together?

Pause. She reappears.

I was thinking on the bus. We're so close to – you know. And it'd be, I dunno, devastating if it were *too* plungey – you know? Whatever happens we'll stay together, won't we, muckers forever?

Hattie Let's just get through / A-levels,

James Because I was thinking we could live in a flat. Or house. Instead of Halls or, you know, when . . . (*Pause.*) We wouldn't need much. If we can't afford glasses and things we can use . . . (*yoghurt pot*) Then if we got jobs playing at hotels or . . . and then if we found two or three other people then maybe along with this (*yoghurt*) and this (*Mateus bottle*) I was thinking maybe we could take *this*. To the house.

Hattie (*pause*) Mum's piano?

James I've dated it to 1910 by the way. (*Plays note.*) I thought she was getting it tuned, see, it's not as if she cares for it, and if she does play she plays like a bitch – *I* don't think – *I* never – *you* called her – I love Mrs B. She was quite off when I rang last night – does she like me? I thought she did but it's not like it was in France.

Hattie Nothing is, the shack's the only place Louise is happy.

James It's funny how you call your mum Louise and your manoir a shack –

Hattie Stop taking things personally, she more than likes you, she *approves*: sweet, polite, perfectly pitched James.

James Oh. I can be rude –

Hattie Mum doesn't give a fuck about any of my friends!

James Well, that's reassuring –

Hattie She loves you, Liberace –

James Could you ask her to stop calling me that?

Hattie – and she loves how much you love her piano, we all do, now come / on –

James This isn't about her piano, it's about us, and it won't be *her* piano, will it, it'll be *yours*, because she's going to give it to *you* when you –

Stops. Silence.

Um, Hattie . . . when you make fun of me for having perfect pitch . . . When I was a kid . . . I had this amazing teacher called Madame Schultz, she died, she was ancient, I got this new one . . . and because I had perfect pitch, he said I was special, and because I was special, he . . .

Silence.

Hattie Madame Schultz?

James She'd fled Germany, she was a genius, I used to go to her house, she lived with her crazy sister, and when I got my new teacher I held on to everything Madame Schultz had taught me because otherwise with Mum gone . . . I wouldn't have been able to . . .

Hattie (*turns tape recorder off*)

James When your school sacked you from *Noye's Fludde*, that was, um . . . the worst thing for me. I hardly knew you, but you were the first person since Madame Schultz who really *got* me. You saved my life . . . so thanks . . .

He shyly kisses her. Silence. She goes to the piano and plays, by heart, with great feeling, Fanny Mendelssohn's Mélodie op. 4, no. 2, as she will in 1999. He is confused.

Hattie I took this to my piano teacher, he said no. What do you think it's about? I think lost love. Isn't it gorgeous?

His bewilderment grows. She continues.

James Was that F-natural a mistake?

She stops. Finds precious sheet music, checks. He is at music with her.

Oh. Must be a misprint. (*Pause.*) So what do you think? About living together?

Hattie I think I'll go to Thailand to help the Cambodians. (*Vodka from piano. She doesn't drink.*) Or India. (*Presses bottle on him.*) Pour it over Mum's cake, the drunker she is the more she'll like you, might say yes to you stealing her grand.

James I'm not suggesting we *steal* – s-so Mrs B *doesn't* like me?

Hattie She thinks you're a deadly cocktail of shy, pretentious, stuck-up and smug. (*Regrets this.*) But she also thinks you deserve everything good that comes to you . . . and she's going to practically push us down the aisle when you tell her you've been awarded a place at the Royal College of Music.

Pause. She removes from his pocket his paperback, out of that, the envelope, out of that, the letter. She reads. Confusion.

Principal study – composition?

James Yeah . . . piano second study. I didn't say, because . . . you know. I applied with two things I've composed. I've always composed – only Mr Simpson knew. He wrote my reference. Honestly, I thought they'd see through my samples, they're a bit . . . Ben Britteny, but they loved them, and my exam day went well. The letter came yesterday, but I didn't know, I was helping the Dragon at church, she knew I'd been waiting and didn't say, it wasn't till I got home, that's why I rang you so late. (*Pause.*) I never dreamt . . . Have you heard yet?

Hattie No. (*Pause.*) It's wonderful, James. Congratulations.

She kisses him on the lips for a long time. She breaks it, physicalises exaggerated excitement, claps, scoops at yoghurt, etc. His confusion intensifies.

I'm glad it's Saturday, I want your input on something. (*Finds tape recorder, presses record.*) Remember that old piece from *my* entrance samples, the *ballade* – starts in A? I played it for you ages ago, more than once, you loved it, you know: (*plays one-fingered phrase of main theme of the familiar melody*)

James Um – ?

Hattie I was thinking. What if this: (*plays piece at its most straightforward, lush and beguiling. Stops on an imperfect/interrupted cadence*) Became this:

Plays a modulation that alters the modality: more rhythmically and harmonically adventurous – as at St Pancras. He watches, not listening. She plays passionately. After a while, a woman enters, the epitome of seventies cool. She is carrying two mugs. James notices her first. Eventually:

Oh my God embarrassing! (*Tries to play it cool; excited teenager keeps erupting.*)

Woman Keep going, you're amazing.

Hattie No I'm crap – we thought you'd want a lie-in.

Woman Yeah, thanks – (*sotto*) quite a hangover.

Hattie giggles – they share a memory. James stares.

Hi, James. I can't believe how much Chrissie's grown.

James Miss Simpson?

Woman Bloody hell, man, 'Miss Simpson', I'm twenty-four not fifty. Eve. Your mum thought you'd both like tea.

Hattie Thanks, Eve, thanks, apparently she's making fairy cakes, let's have fairy cakes.

Eve Yeah, I don't eat flour and even if I did I couldn't face cake. I should go.

Hattie (*uncool*) Oh no no no, you have to stay! – (*cool*) stay.

Eve I think I should get out of your family's hair . . . (*intimate, re: clothes*) and change . . . but listen, do you want to meet later?

Hattie (*uncool*) Cool! (*Cool.*) Cool.

Eve Maybe come by in an hour or two? Some friends are going to a gig at a pub tonight if you want to come, but we could have the afternoon together first?

Hattie Yes, cool! Yes.

A moment. They kiss. Silence.

Eve Tag along if you like, James. Bloody hell, man, *Noye's Fludde*, what was my brother thinking doing that, those poor kids – hymns, teacups,

Hattie It was his fault! He foisted his idiosyncratic taste on three whole schools!

Eve That's right – yeah, man, maybe *Joseph and the Dreamcoat* next time? (*Squawking.*) 'The jism of / the flood –'

Hattie joins in, plinking the mugs, they laugh. Silence. Eve sees the Kate Bush LP.

You listened?

Hattie Thank you *so* much.

Eve 'Oh to Be in Love'.

Hattie I know!

Eve 'You crush the lily in my soul.'

Hattie I *know*!

Silence.

Eve Well . . . thanks for . . . [bed]. I'll see you later? Twelvish?

Hattie I'll see you out! (*Grabs her hand.*)

Eve Bye, James.

James Bye, Miss Simpson.

They leave, laughing (about him). He is stock-still. An impossibly long pause. He drinks vodka. She returns, licking the bowl. Plays a few notes.

Hattie Want some?

James C-can you please wipe your hands before you [play]. (*Pause.*) So how long have you been friends with Noah's Wife?

Hattie Um – since *Noye's Fludde*. On and off. Yesterday I just rang and said, time you met my parents. Got so late. So drunk. She's teaching me to meditate.

James Is she?

Hattie She's a Buddhist. But angry.

James About Pol Pot?

Hattie Yes, she's very passionate. Have you read *Rubyfruit Jungle*?

James Have you?

Hattie Have you read *The Bluest Eye*? Have you seen *Jules et Jim*?

James We went to *Jules and Jim* together / in –

Hattie You know, you should get angry more often, James.

James I'm not angry.

Hattie Good, because it's not as if I've hidden anything from you, ever.

Puts bowl on piano. It bothers him.

James You'll get an offer.

Hattie I won't, I fucked up my exam day, and if I do, I'll turn it down.

James You can't go to India, Hattie, you can do that in a few years –

Hattie Thanks, careers officer, and I'm going to Venice, Eve's shooting a film there –

James Eve! –

Hattie I'm never going to live in a fleapit in South Kensington with you, all right?! It's fine, it's okay, I've decided I'm going to the Royal College of *Life*.

Turns record player on, drops stylus. Mid-song: 'Wuthering Heights'. Dances a bit. A few lyrics. For herself, her own world – meaningful to her, not silly. He watches. Great pain in her face. Turns volume up. Now, once or twice, her moves goad him, as they will in 1999. He turns the music off. Silence.

I have news too. I basically didn't go to bed last night because – so Eve works at the BBC, yeah? And things are very Women's Lib there, all kinds of composers, electronic, mainly – like Delia Derbyshire, you know, *Doctor Who*, and Daphne Oram – who told the Royal College of Music to sod off – and a while back Eve told me to – give her a tape – and – turns out they want this *ballade*. My piece. The BBC. I called it 'The Cusp of Life', it's just for one of their information films, you know those *Protect and Survive* nuclear war things – Cusp of Death, Cusp of Soviet Annihilation. Just for a tiny fallout shelter scene or something, that's why I want your thoughts: I want to smash it so I can rebuild it, and separately I have ideas for lyrics, because I think it's songs for me actually, like Kate, like Joni, you know?

James (*pause*) That A-major thing?

Hattie It starts in A.

James The BBC? Just like that? What, you have a contract?

Hattie Not yet but they're going to pay.

James How much?

Hattie I don't know, eighty quid or something.

James (*noise!*)

Hattie It's not much, but it's not nothing and it might lead to something. It's just a public information – forget it.

Busies herself. He stares.

James Mrs Arbuthnot said Miss Simpson's a BBC teagirl.

Hattie No, she said secretary and Arbuthnot's a self-loathing crab. Eve's an independent filmmaker and to earn money she's a script kind of – she works on the / public –

James Right, so did Miss Simpson say over her Pernod last night that the BBC *might* be interested in your piece which you haven't even sent to her – or are they *actually* interested in it?

Hattie Stop acting like I've stabbed you in the back. I haven't: but you have. (*Re: his letter.*) Composition? And what the fuck? Move in with you? What, to have babies or something? (*Stares.*) Oh my God.

James You've had a letter. Since we're killing the thing we love, let's do it honestly.

83

Hattie I know who that is. That's Oscar Wilde! You really are / something!

James What do your parents think of you not / going to –

Hattie Who cares, it's my life! Something's happened, okay? Someone likes my stuff and made something happen, so just be happy. You should probably go.

James I don't / want to –

Hattie Also if we're to continue to be friends you need to stop calling your stepmother Dragon. I know she'll never replace your mother but she feeds you and buys you clothes and gave you a *sister* –

James *Half* and-and you hate your mother, you called / her a –

Hattie (*at precious sheet music*) Why do you think this F-natural's a misprint? (*Plays bar 15, with F-sharp, then F-natural.*) It's what Fanny Mendelssohn wrote. (*Pause.*) Every weekend you come here and we 'shag' and you lecture me on 'Balinese influences' in the works of the composers you love –

James I don't lecture, and I thought you liked / talking –

Hattie I do, but the fact is you always *sneer* at my choices: Lili, Clara: 'makes no difference –'

James *You* sneer at everything *I* love –

Hattie Only because you won't acknowledge what *really* speaks to you in it! It's so blatant: in *Death in Venice* Aschenbach *chooses* not to tell the boy's mother there's a deadly plague because the horny old fucker *wants the boy to stay*! I was at *Noye's Fludde* for five minutes and Miss Simpson's changed my life – you haven't had the guts to tell Charlie Tyler you fancy him in five *years*. You've no idea how lucky you are, how much there is for you to esteem. So stop sneering at my wives and sisters because they're all I've got. You quote Wilde at me, but you shrivel up when Mum calls

84

you Liberace because you're too terrified to go anywhere near what Britten's *actually about*, what Wilde *did* and *suffered* to beat a *path for you*.

Silence.

I'm not your girlfriend. Or exclusively yours. I love you . . . mostly how weird you are. You need to accept what that is, it's *not nothing*, it's why you have that letter, they've seen something in you, you play fantastic, turns out you compose fantastic, so just grab it, grab what's *special* about *you*.

Works on her recognisable music. He is still.

James Mrs Arbuthnot said you'd do this to me.

Hattie (*stops*) I'm really sorry my being sacked hurt *you* so much that you haven't had one second to consider how much I loved *Noye's Fludde* and *wanted to play it*.

Silence.

Go. You dirty snitch.

James What?

Hattie The jealousy's beginning to stink.

Works. He is still.

James Me? Jealous of this? This is why you didn't get in.

Hattie Well, the BBC wants it.

James You don't have to make up a lie to stop me from thinking you're a failure when –

Hattie You already think it?

Heads off. He stops her with a hideous chord. He dismantles the tune along these lines:

James It's not the worst thing ever written, but . . . dominant to tonic, what a surprising interval. And this leitmotif, (*the recognisable melody*) if I can use a German word for something so Home Counties. Then it's just a modulation to the relative minor, yeah? Like a wedding cake with diminishing layers. There's no point 'remaking' it, it's dead on arrival. So I know you're lying. Why would the BBC want to show people how to build fallout shelters to this Blancmange in A-major? That's why the College rejected you – they're looking for potential and there's no beginning to yours.

He is immediately wretched, apologetic. Silence.

Hattie I wrote that piece for you.

James (*shakes head*)

Hattie The title's you. *Noye's Fludde*'s about being on 'the c-cusp of life', you said. Who says things like that? *Only a* FUCKING QUEER LIKE YOU.

Opens piano stool, throws fragments of her letter at him. It's raining. She sits, similarly wretched. Plays a note. Can't continue. He sits beside her. He plays the music, lush and beguiling. Chrissie enters, unseen. She listens, enchanted. After a while, Hattie closes the lid on him. He tries to hold her – for a moment she yields, but pushes him off.

Chrissie Jamie?

Hattie rushes out.

James Get out.

Chrissie You're crying. I saw Noah's Wife.

James Go away,

He can't show his face. She is tearful.

Chrissie I liked the music. Did you write it for Hats?

He notices the tape recorder, and is upset by all it has recorded. He ejects the tape and puts it in his cardigan pocket. Glugs a fair amount of vodka. Grabs raincoat. Has second thoughts about the tape and takes it out to return it –

Where are you going? Can I play?

Hattie enters to collect cigarettes – refreshed hair, bag, car keys – as he snaps:

James Why are you so stupid, Chrissie, you should have gone with your fucking mother today –(*immediate regret. Seeing Hattie, he must slip tape back in his pocket*)

Chrissie Hats, can I play the piano?

Hattie You're going home now.

Chrissie I don't want to!

Hattie Well, you have to.

Chrissie Jamie didn't mean it, why are you fighting, he wrote the music for you!

Hugs her. Silence.

I don't want to walk to the bus in the rain! (*Goes to piano, picks out a few notes, redolent of the music.*)

Hattie Stop it. (*To James.*) Stop her. (*To Chrissie.*) I said stop, get out!

James Don't talk to her like that –

Chrissie I forgot our umbrella, I don't want to! What's happened?

Slams piano shut. The hand-bells that introduce Noye's Fludde's *final hymn are heard.*

Hattie I'm going to my girlfriend Eve's. I'll drop you both home on my way, okay?

Chrissie In your car? Yes! Yes, let's go, Jamie, come on, hurry, let's go!

The child runs away. The hand-bells ring. She appears in the window, excitedly putting on her red duffel coat, and the distant, timeless children sing 'The spacious firmament on high' as she jumps up and down and shouts, unheard: 'Hurry! Jamie! Hats! Let's go, let's go, let's go!' The piano

*is still, an antique hall bench appears, the hymn fades to
the hum of people in another room. James, holding a cup
of tea, is staring at the piano.*

Hattie Here you are. Perfect – I'll go and get her.

James You kept it?

Hattie Yes?

James I never assumed that.

Hattie Why not? Tell me you're happy to see it.

James I never knew if I'd done a good or arrogant thing.

Hattie Oh. Both. James. How could anyone resent being
reunited with their childhood piano?

James No, I never presumed that had happened, not once in
sixteen years.

Hattie But surely you knew we'd collected it?

James Yes, the dealer confirmed that, but . . . (*emotional*)
I knew the night of that concert all contact was off, so . . .
I didn't know if it had been *kept*, or . . . sorry . . .

His hand shakes: the teacup rattles in its saucer. She waits.

So she played it, did she, Frances? Hats played it?

Frances (*that is, the actor who plays Hattie*) It's funny to
hear you call Mum Hats. No one called her that. She was
always Hattie. Of course she did. She never filmed in this
room, this was her sanctuary. (*Rescues his tea, puts it on
piano.*) I'll bring you some food. Play something if you want.

James Oh no, I don't anymore, perhaps we should both go
back to the party –

Frances Is that what it's called, party?

James I never know – and these days I go to a funeral
a week –

Retrieves the vexing teacup: she stares: it roots him there. He shakes.

It was kind of you to invite me, Frances. Hattie must have been proud of you. Your eulogy was perfect, though I spent most of it wondering how you could be thirty-eight – *thirty-eight*!

Laughs so hard the tea is threatened again. She takes it, puts it on the bench –

Frances The question is what are *you* doing for your eightieth?

James Oh, bag of crisps at the pub if I'm lucky.

Frances (*pause*) I'll get Ma.

James Frances!? (*Pause.*) Do you play?

Frances Obviously there wasn't much music when I was growing up. By the time of St Pancras I was at uni. Maybe I can still – (*Bangs opening of 'Für Elise'.*) Why would that evil tune flow across my synapses when I've forgotten all my Italian lessons?

James (*pauses, moved*) It's a lovely tune. It's familiar, that's all. Do you know *Death in Venice* – no reason you should – there's the story, opera, film, and . . . paradox, but each is the perfect version. The opera's my desert island music, but nothing in it moves me like a scene in the film where the boy plays Beethoven's 'Für Elise'.

Frances Well, along with this it's my entire repertoire:

Plays a grisly burst of 'Chopsticks' on which Bo enters, with a plate of food.

Bo Isn't there one room in my own house where I can eat a sausage roll in peace?

Frances Ma – I was coming to get you.

Bo sits on the bench, eats. Frances is seated patiently at the piano.

James I never dreamt I'd be . . . destroyed by Kate Bush. But she destroyed me today. (*Pause.*) I really thought she'd sell it. The odd thing, Frances, is that I can count on one hand the times your mother and I have seen each other since we were young, yet she is *the* person in my / life –

Frances It's a rule here if we're talking about my mothers we make clear which one.

James Oh I don't need a whole hand for Bo either do I, Bo? – Yvonne – three fingers'll do – and with each she's hated me more.

Frances Ma doesn't hate you, no one hates you.

Bo Don't assume that, Frances – what is that anyway, old man, Parkinson's?

James No. Terror.

Bo chuckles, Frances smiles. For the rest of the scene, Frances plays fragments.

Frances I invited you because I wanted to. When Mum first told me everything, I wanted to cancel the hell out of you but she wouldn't let us because of your stepmother. Then by the time you told us she'd died, Mum had grabbed who she really was anyway. She never wanted you on the end of a mob. Because you were there together. When you lost your sister.

James . . . there was . . . shouting in the car . . . we were both upset, shouting . . . then,

He has to sit. Bo offers food. He takes a morsel.

I've forgotten many things. But I remembered that serial number like I remember so much music. And I knew when I worked on that film, I knew. My first husband would have psychoanalysed this, others have: like any music I took it deep inside, but then I denied Hattie – but what's just as shameful is I didn't do her music justice. Everyone played those public pianos, she went viral because her piece had

wonders that my – wh-what I mean is my version's *nothing*,
so it's a double crime, to think I was better than her *and* steal
from her, and *still* not honour her. When I found that cassette
and heard myself tear her music apart, it was shame on
shame . . . when I gave her the cassette and this (*re: piano*),
I never assumed I was forgiven, perhaps you believe that,
I thought she'd expose me to the world that night,

Bo Enough.

James One thing's consoled me, Yvonne. I had this studio in
the City, she turned up pissed, broke my Christmas tree,
actually poured vodka in my . . . I *wish* I'd been honest that
day, her friend, but if I *had* . . . when you met she told you
she'd been to an interview, but I think she'd been with me, in
her two scarves, so you see, she met *you*. (*Pause.*) We were
meant to play together in *Noye's* . . . I missed my poor little
sister, I wanted them both back,

Bo Will you take the piano for us?

James What? No, it's yours, Frances's –

Bo Her children play guitar. It needs to go, I'm selling this
house. Shaking and verbal diarrhoea aside, you seem quite
well.

James I worked on a strawberry farm for ten years. I'm on
my third husband.

Bo Find someone who'll love it, get your money back.

James Oh I'll never get back what I paid for that fucking
thing.

Bo Glad to hear it. Well, you'll get what it's worth. You can
buy some new trousers.

> *Arresting change: the date rewinds – from 2039 – and
> Hattie is performing – spotlight, microphone – climaxing
> a ballad redolent of 'Oranges and Lemons' with the lyric
> 'the day of St Clement's and Bo'. Bo and James remain on*

the bench, as if in an audience, watching. Before the song's
final chord, Hattie speaks into the microphone.

WELCOME TO THE ROYAL FESTIVAL HALL
11 APRIL 2024   20.45

Hattie That was a song for my wife and daughter . . .

Applause from the supportive audience, and immediately
she begins the oscillating semitones. This prompts
recognition, excitement. The date and time remain.

Thanks for coming tonight. When I was young I never once
dreamt of playing here.

Laughter.

You *can't* want St Pancras?

They do. But she stops. Uneasy silence.

I started playing after a long break – you know that. But it
was only today, in my dressing room before . . . that I found
the words for what I'd circled back to, for the feeling,
I mean. Playing, writing again, I feel like . . . I've scaled an
Alp, like a young, wandering, y'know, German. And on the
cusp of her life . . . with her . . . *Italy* right there . . . she turns
round . . . and sees you.

Light narrows on James.

With your shit tattoo. Seventies side parting. NHS specs. And
all she wants to say,

Silence.

is that you can hold on, to the little girl in your kitchen. Or
you can say, gently, so she understands: time to go. So I'm
not going to play this tonight or ever again. I listened to
what you gave me, we both come out of it badly, no one else
will ever hear it – because why? Why when you're in row C,
and I'm here, with new music, mine. I love you, and maybe
I'm here because of us, and I think our lives go further back

92

than we know, but don't contact me again – I'm sixty-fucking-three, motherfuckers, I've got arthritis, I play like a church-lady organist, but I have this *one* window, this *last, tiny time* and it's *mine*.

Arresting change: the date remains as the time alone rewinds

11 APRIL 2024   17.08

and magically the bench yields James his satchel and he takes the package out and makes Bo take it as she disappears and Hattie sits next to him

2020

and they laugh, old friends, he reaches for her hand and it dies,

James Why? Why did you play?

and the sounds of the station and passengers, and Bo is seen with take-away coffees

WELCOME TO ST PANCRAS INTERNATIONAL

and Hattie is playing the beguiling tune, Commuters filming, and her hands rise but the music continues in a disturbingly jagged orchestral version

1999

and she is dancing, in her own world, la-la-ing at James, the music so loud we can't hear, until he leaves and she is in the midst of terrifying traffic and Bo rushes to her and City bells chime and 'Hark! The Herald Angels Sing' on a church organ plays and James returns and Bo disappears and everything cuts to uncanny silence and

1978

Hattie It's wonderful, James. Congratulations,

1977

James This is a massive manoir, not a shack.

93

Hattie (*laughs*) It's the summer of our lives, Piggy, *c'est l'été de nos vies.*

1976

James Have we met?

Hattie No: you're unforgettable,

and Chrissie in her school uniform tears towards the piano, and it is on the move

1966

and stops in the depths of a house, where a piano teacher is teaching a Girl with the appearance of Chrissie who is stumbling her way through a simple piece. Hattie, in a blazer, with a satchel, is on the antique bench in the hall. A red duffel coat is next to her. The bench must have grown because her feet can't reach the ground. James, in a different blazer, with his satchel, has just arrived. He is very shy.

Who are you?

James No one.

Hattie What time's your lesson?

James A quarter past four.

Hattie That's my time! Run and tell your mother at once.

James My mummy's . . . Daddy dropped me here.

Hattie Go and tell him!

James He's gone.

Hattie Go and tell Madame Schultz's sister! You're early or late!

He obeys. She waits, swinging legs, giggling at Girl's mistakes. He returns.

James She told me to wait. Should I tell Madame Schultz?

Hattie Goodness no, she's in a lesson!

He stands there. Shyly lifts himself on bench. His feet can't reach the floor. They wait.

(*Secret.*) Mummy says Madame Schultz's sister's crazy. But it's because she's very sad but what if all the music in their house makes the sadness worse? How old are you?

James Six.

Hattie I'm six and a half.

James I'm six and three-quarters.

Hattie Maybe Madame Schultz will have the lesson after mine with someone else and you won't even have one.

He bites his nails. She produces a chocolate bar.

You can't have my lesson, she's very expensive.

James She came from Germany.

Hattie Yes, but she calls herself 'Madame' because that's what artists do. Maybe your daddy's gone forever.

James Maybe your mummy's gone forever.

Hattie (*clapping*) Hope so, Louise is always – (*Gestures drinking: learned from an adult.*) Do you want some Bounty?

James No, I don't want to get Madame Schultz's Steinway dirty.

Hattie Goody two shoes, we have a Bechstein, we don't care about that.

Eats. After a bit, he snatches the chocolate. She hits him, hard. He gives it back. Silence. They are adults.

James I'm sorry.

Silence.

Hattie I know.

Silence. Madame Schultz approaches briskly with Girl, who puts on the duffel coat.

Madame Schultz (*calls*) Sara, is Cynthia's mother here?! Wait for her, Cynthia, find my sister if you need the lavatory. What are you doing here, James?

Hattie His daddy got the time wrong, Madame Schultz.

Madame Schultz But I told that nice Rosamund who's staying with you that you're at five. Never mind, there's been a confusion, I know things aren't easy for you all.

Hattie Why?

Madame Schultz Don't be nosy, Hattie. (*To James.*) Study the Bach. Come along. (*Leads her to piano room; re: precious sheet music.*) You're to put this in your satchel and study it this week. Protect with your life, it's by Fanny Hensel, sister of Felix – wipe your filthy hands, young lady!

Girl and James wait on the bench. Hattie plays scales. Doorbell. Girl runs off. Hattie plays 'Für Elise'. It's wonderfully fluent. James is drawn towards the piano-room door. He listens. Moved. Consoled. Wants to leave. Bites nails. Doesn't want to leave. Wants to be able to play like Hattie. The woman who is all the women but Hattie passes in front of him.

ELKE SCHULTZ, CONCERT PIANIST AND TEACHER,
1893–1966, 73 YEARS

JEAN ARBUTHNOT, NÉE INGLES, TEACHER,
1919–1995, 76 YEARS

EVE SIMPSON, TELEVISION PRODUCTION ASSISTANT,
1955–1982, 27 YEARS

LOUISE BUCHANAN, 1943–2006, 63 YEARS

ROSAMUND CULLER, MBE, NÉE GARVEY,
CHARITY OFFICER, 1945–2024, 78 YEARS

Bo is still.

PROFESSOR YVONNE 'BO' JOHN, ACADEMIC,
1957–2051, 94 YEARS

She leaves.

JAMES CULLER, COMPOSER AND TEACHER,
1960–2040, 80 YEARS

He leaves.

HATTIE BUCHANAN,
TAX INSPECTOR AND SINGER-SONGWRITER,
1960–2039, 79 YEARS

Her hands rise but the music continues. She leaves. The semitones of 'Für Elise' become the ballad of Hattie,

CHRISTINA CULLER, 1970–1978

which continues.

Appendix

In the event of music-rights clearance issues, the long stage direction on p. 72 can be replaced with the following:

Hattie appears to be playing as Bo leaves and James is left alone with the hum of the foyer and the children's distant, timeless singing. The sounds build, the piano is on the move, and James disappears as it stops in the room with a window to a rainy street, where Hattie is holding an LP cover (The Kick Inside), *and, via headphones connected to a record player on the piano, is listening to some song, digging it, sounding the odd indecipherable note/word: teenage ecstasy. Also on piano: other LPs, sheet music, a candle in a Mateus Rosé bottle. Inspired, she puts the cover down and writes feverishly on manuscript. She turns the LP off and removes from the stool the tape recorder, inserts tape, hits record, eats yoghurt, plays the oscillating semitones. Doorbell. She is surprised. Looks at her watch. Swears. Wonders what to do. Climbs on piano, poses provocatively. Enter James – cardigan, raincoat, satchel, wiping his glasses.*

and the sequence after James's 'I'm not angry' on p. 82 can be replaced with the following:

Hattie Good, because it's not as if I've hidden anything from you, ever.

Puts plate on piano. It bothers him. She removes LP, finds another, flicks record player on.

James You'll get an offer.

Hattie I won't, I fucked up my exam day, and if I do, I'll turn it down.

James You can't go to India, Hattie, you can do that in a few years –

Hattie Thanks, careers officer, and I'm going to Venice, Eve's shooting a film there –

James Eve! –

Hattie I'm never going to live in a fleapit in South Kensington with you, all right?! It's fine, it's okay, I've decided I'm going to the Royal College of *Life*.

Drops stylus. Mid-song: Fanny Mendelssohn's 'Italien' (no. 3 of Felix's op. 8). Dances a bit. A few mangled German words. For herself, her own world – meaningful to her, not silly. He watches. Great pain in her face. Turns volume up. Now, once or twice, her moves goad him, as they will in 1999. He turns it off. Silence.